How to Be
Happy
in an
Unhappy World

How to Be Happy in an Unhappy World

by

ARNOLD PRATER

THOMAS NELSON PUBLISHERS
Nashville • Camden • New York

Published in Nashville, Tennessee, by Thomas Nelson, Inc. and distributed in Canada by Lawson Falle, Ltd., Cambridge, Ontario.

Printed in the United States of America.

The Scripture quotations in this publication are from the *Revised Standard Version* of the Bible, copyrighted 1946, 1952, © 1971, 1973 by the Division of Christian Education of the National Council of the Churches of Christ in the U.S.A., and are used by permission.

Scripture quotations marked KJV are from the *King James Version* of the Bible.

Scripture quotations marked *Good News* are from the *Good News Bible*—New Testament: Copyright © American Bible Society 1966, 1971, 1976.

Library of Congress Cataloging in Publication Data

Prater, Arnold.
    Hot to be happy in an unhappy world.

    1. Christian life—Methodist authors.   2. Happiness.
I. Title.
BV4501.2.P657   1983   248.4   83-17373
ISBN 0-8407-5866-9 (pbk.)

For Dr. Robert G. Mayfield
and Dr. Frank Bateman Stanger,
men of God,
full of the Holy Spirit,
and my brothers in Christ,
who have done more for me
and for the kingdom of God
than they will ever know
this side of eternity.

Contents

How to Be
Happy
in an
Unhappy World

1

If You Found It,
Would You Recognize It?

She sat in my office with head bowed, her eyebrows forming two deep slashes of concern in her forehead. Her cheeks were glistening from her tears. But now her sobs had subsided, and she breathed a long sigh of resignation and hopelessness.

"I'm just not happy anymore," she said.

But I knew she had never been happy. She had been married for about six months and had given every appearance of basking in super-happiness, but she was not. She had only bought a ticket to Fantasyland and had wandered through its enchanting streets, exotic shops, and ice-cream parlors for a few months.

Now she had to depart through the gates of reality, and the change of atmosphere was so abrupt that she panicked because she thought she had lost happiness.

Poor girl, she thought she could trap Fantasyland in a box, carry it to a beautiful vacant lot somewhere, unfold the box, and build a dream house into which happiness would constantly flow like the cooling breezes from an air-conditioning system.

She thought she could control it all with the thermostat of her desire—if things got a bit dull or the excitement simmered down, she could just reach inside herself and turn up her happiness until it reached the comfort zone again.

What was wrong? She was a Christian and she loved her husband, so that was not the problem. She loved God, and *He* certainly could not be the problem. She was a faithful seeker in the Word, so the Bible could not be the problem. Thus, the only intelligent conclusion she could reach was that *she* was the problem.

It was an accurate conclusion.

Although it took a few more sessions until she began to understand her dilemma, I knew the answer to her problem from the beginning, not because I was especially wisdom-filled but simply because I had been through the very same experience myself.

She was looking for the wrong thing.

I have been saying it for years, and I want to say it again now. If you are looking for a faith that will keep you up on Cloud Nine all the time, forget it! If you find such an ecstatic state in some sort of religion or another, don't trust it—for it won't be Christianity.

Did our Lord Jesus live on Cloud Nine all the time? Well, they sought to kill Him before He was sixty days old. From the day He began His ministry they dogged His steps daily. They hung out on the edge of the crowd like hovering vultures, waiting for Him to make a slip.

They arrested Him on trumped-up political charges, tried Him in courts that were illegal and a sham. Finally a weak-kneed ruler, as a matter of political expediency, sacrificed his own convictions and gave Him up to them.

They dragged Him off outside the city to an ugly little hill shaped like death itself, and "there they crucified him" (Luke 23:33). Remember now, they were doing all this to *God*, the Lord Jesus Christ Himself. His first cry from the cross was not for Himself but for those who did Him in.

He had made the very tree upon which He was hung. He had deposited in the earth the iron ore from which the spear was made that pierced His side, and the nails that held Him there. He scattered the seeds that produced the bush from which was fashioned His crown of thorns.

He groaned aloud that He was thirsty, yet it was He who had poured out every cooling mountain stream; indeed, every river on earth including the mighty Amazon, a hundred miles wide at its mouth.

He cried in agony at His aloneness, for at that point He was forsaken by heaven, denied by earth, and placarded in between. Finally, between two felons, He bowed His great head and died.

How in the name of heaven can anyone expect to take the faith of that God-man, dilute it with some kind of Ponce de León mixture, and make of it a religion that will keep us floating along on some good angel's wings through day after day of perfect bliss and heavenly manna?

Yet I submit to you that Jesus Christ was the happiest, most radiant personality ever to set foot on this wayside, wayward planet!

So you're not happy? Then perhaps you, too, like the frustrated young woman in my office, have been looking for the wrong thing. Perhaps you, too, have somehow become confused.

Did you think that after you found Christ life would be without problems (or at least without *as many* problems as you had before)? Did you think you'd never have the blues, or be discouraged, or be terribly tempted? That the enemy would see the sign of the cross upon you and not harass you as much as he does others? That God would always seem precious and near, that your prayers would never seem to bounce off the ceiling like so many carnival balloons?

It hasn't worked out that way, has it?

So you're asking, "What went wrong? I certainly missed the boat somewhere. I surely must not be a very 'good' Christian or things would be different."

Well, have I got news for you—good news! There's probably not that much wrong; you may be happy and not even know it! Before this chapter ends I'll explain what I mean by that. But first let me suggest that a part of all this confusion about what it means to be happy in an unhappy world has arisen because we have confused what the world says about happiness with what the Word of God says about it—and they are two vastly different things.

We hear the word "happiness" kicked around so much that it has laser-beamed our unconscious minds into thinking that happiness can be *anything* material. Here are some worldly definitions I have read very recently.

"Happiness is owning a _____ (automobile)."

"Happiness is a trip to our cheese bar."

"Happiness is a new hairdo by _____ (beautician's name)."

"Happiness is being a size 10 within sixty days!"

"Happiness is seeing your puppy free from worms."

I don't need to go on; you have seen them too. And every bar in America advertises a "happy hour" each afternoon.

We have been deceived into thinking that happiness is always strictly *feeling*. That is surely one of the biggest lies ever to come from the big guns of the adversary. Only yesterday the mail brought a long letter from a dear Christian woman whose faith is radiant. Yet in writing about a spiritual problem she said, "Sometimes I just feel like I am not doing enough for God." The unwritten remainder of that sentence would have to be, "so if I could just just do more for Him my unhappy feelings would disappear."

We will be dealing with what to do about feelings a bit later, but for now let me assure you that trying to measure true happiness by feelings is a short-fused firecracker that will explode in our faces every time.

We have spoken about what the world has to say about happiness, and we said the Bible has something different to say. So it is time to stop right here, mix some spiritual cement, and lay down a foundation fact upon which we will build everything else from here on in. That fact is that there are two definite and distinct kinds of happiness. There is (A) *circumstantial happiness*, which is always emotional, and there is (B) *spiritual happiness*, which also touches our emotions but is constant. Type B does not vary; it is always present within. Sometimes it may be combined with Type A, but it is not ultimately dependent upon it.

Type A is *always* temporary; it never lasts. It may appear as a result of many things, but the things that produce it are also temporary. It is always sensory and therefore has its origins in the material. Anything that is sensory or material is subject to change.

But Type B is spiritual; it has its origin in the Holy Spirit and therefore is *never* temporary but eternal. It abides because the Holy Spirit abides. There is no variation in it because there is none in God (see James 1:17).

Where does the Holy Spirit abide? In the human spirit. You see, we are tripartite beings. God's Word confirms this in Paul's benediction in 1 Thessalonians 5:23:

> May the God of peace himself sanctify you wholly; and may your spirit and soul and body be kept sound and blameless at the coming of our Lord Jesus Christ.

"Soul" and "spirit" may be used interchangeably. So it may be said we are spirit beings who *have* a mind and who *live* in a body. The spirit is the part of us that is eternal; it is the part of us for which Jesus died. From the spirit all communication with God arises and is fed to us through our minds, where it touches our emotions.

But we know and worship God in our spirits. Jesus said as much:

> The hour is coming, and now is, when the true worshipers will worship the Father in spirit and truth, for such the Father seeks to worship him (John 4:23).

We *love* God with our minds and our spirits, but we *know* Him in our spirits, by faith. So *spiritual happiness* originates when the Holy Spirit conveys to our spirits what we need to know above and beyond our circumstances. That is the "spring of water welling up" within us (John 4:14). The Spirit is the witness who confirms what we believe by faith. ("He who believes in the Son of God has the testimony in himself" 1 John 5:10.) But *circumstantial happiness* originates in the mind.

Now let's put that in biscuit-and-gravy terms. Circumstantial happiness is almost self-explanatory. It is, to put it simply, "feeling good" about something. You get an unexpected kiss from your husband; you see the first jonquil in the springtime; your son comes home from the armed forces; you sit down to a T-bone steak; there is an unexpected long-distance call from a loved one—and you just "feel good." You're emotionally happy, and that is not a bad thing; in fact, most of the time it's great! We need all of it we can get!

But spiritual happiness goes far beyond any of

those things, although it does reach our emotions.

Spiritual happiness is not a thing to be achieved, a goal to be reached. Rather, it is always a *by-product* of something else. No, let me say it better: it is a by-product of *Someone* else—the Holy Spirit of God. He is that real, living presence in your heart and life who "will never fail you nor forsake you" (Heb. 13:5).

When you back off from any circumstance, good or bad, and look deeply, you will find He is there and you will know it.

In childhood we used to visit my uncle's farm. In the front yard there was a deep well, about three feet wide. It was covered with an ivy-clad roof, from which hung a bucket. Today it would look like a picture postcard from another day, or a prop on a movie set.

They had dug the well until they struck a slowly moving underground stream. From it we actually caught little fish using bent pin hooks. We leaned over the side and shaded our eyes to try to see in its depths. It was pitch black down in the well, but if we shaded our eyes long enough we could make out the faint reflection of the water. It shimmered like a straying sunbeam that had gotten lost and was struggling to get out. And we knew the river was there!

I'm saying that no matter what kind of hurricane is raging upon the surfaces of life, when you stop in the midst of it and take what I call the "deep-well look," peering way down there through the darkness to the heart core of life where the real you lives, you can always see the glimmer that is the presence of the Lord of life in you—and you are sustained.

And you go on, not just to cope but to conquer!

That's spiritual happiness. That's Type B. It is God's gift to you, His very own power and presence. And you can drink strength and comfort from that River, for He is always there.

That is not some neat idea I invented in my study. Your Lord Jesus made that promise to you, and He said it like this:

> Whoever drinks of the water that I shall give him will never thirst; the water that I shall give him will become *in him* a spring of water welling up to eternal life (John 4:14, italics mine).

I call it the "water-well promise"!

I learned something new from the Creation story the other day. (I'm *always* learning something new from it. Wow! I wonder if there's any bottom to its depths!)

I began reading the second chapter of Genesis and suddenly a phrase exploded like a brilliant star shell, illuminating the awareness centers of my mind with the bright glory of new truth comprehended.

God had just finished the Creation, had seen that it was very "good," and then the Word says, "and he *rested* on the seventh day from all his work which he had done" (Gen. 2:2, italics mine).

What? God rested? Was He tired, worn-out, exhausted from all that work? Well, of course not. God does not get tired. His "body" is not the type that must have a proper diet and eight hours of sleep every night. So what does that verse mean?

I believe that the eternal and everlasting Light moved into the darkness that "was upon the face of the deep," that God Himself moved across those waters of deep nothingness, and that from the exact center of His perfect will and plan He simply commanded and spoke the creation into existence.

Eight times God spoke in creating the form, the substance, the creatures, and finally man himself. Then God "rested" over the entire creation. He found perfect and absolute security in His inner being over what He had done; He "rested" in the sufficiency of His own adequacy.

Spiritual happiness is the fallout from that same kind of inner security. It is God's gift to us, and whoever has that at the heartpath of his life is blessed of God! The Lord Jesus said it like this:

> My peace I give to you; not as the world gives do I give to you. Let not your hearts be troubled, neither let them be afraid (John 14:27).

You cannot live on Cloud Nine, but whenever you want to step back out of the circumstances and take that "deep-well look," you will find that river flowing. You will know that Christ *is* that River and that He Himself lives in you and that He is the complete Lord of the outcome.

Is this some kind of formula for self-induced escape from reality? Does it *really* work in this unhappy world amidst all the strident voices and tragic circumstances of our day?

Dear friends, it's real — and during trying times is when it works the very best. A pastor friend told of one of the members of his congregation. When she was far advanced in years she fell and broke her hip. Doctors in her home town of Ashland, Kentucky, advised that she go to a large medical center in Columbus, Ohio, where newer techniques for replacing hip sockets had been learned. Some of her children objected.

"But, Mother," they said, "it is so far and we have our jobs here and can't go with you. What if something happened to you away over there?"

The mother's brown eyes snapped and she replied, "Well, I talked that over with the Lord and He told me it isn't any farther to heaven from Columbus than it is from Ashland!" And that settled that.

She had taken the deep-well look and found all the spiritual happiness she needed to see her through. The River in her still flowed.

Blessed of God, resting, the inner *knowing* —that's spiritual happiness.

It is more than mere coincidence that the Beatitudes in the *Good News* version of the Bible are worded like this:

Happy are those who know they are
    spiritually poor;
  the Kingdom of heaven belongs to them!
Happy are those who mourn;
  God will comfort them!
Happy are those who are humble;
  they will receive what God has promised!
Happy are those whose greatest desire is to do
    what God requires;
  God will satisfy them fully!

21

Happy are those who are merciful to others;
  God will be merciful to them!
Happy are the pure in heart;
  they will see God!
Happy are those who work for peace;
  God will call them his children!
Happy are those who are persecuted because they
  do what God requires;
    the Kingdom of heaven belongs to them!
Happy are you when people insult you and persecute you and tell all kinds of evil lies against you
  because you are my followers. Be happy and
  glad, for a great reward is kept for you in
  heaven. This is how the prophets who lived
  before you were persecuted (Matt. 5:3-12).

Now look back over these and think through them. In each one you may substitute the phrase "spiritually happy" without damaging the meaning. People who believe God's promises with all their hearts experience Type B—spiritual happiness.

It is certainly different from simple circumstantial happiness. "Mourning" or being "persecuted" or being "insulted" are hardly Cloud Nine circumstances. The message of the Beatitudes is that people in those situations are blessed of God *now* by the hope of promised things yet to come.

But I would not have you think that the basis for my conviction is all secondhand. I am writing out of the depths of my own life.

The phone rang after I had written three pages of this first chapter. It was our daughter Judy, who lives in Florida. She told us that in the middle of the afternoon, six-month-old Jesse, our second grandson, had suddenly developed severe symptoms of alarming illness. Judy had taken him at once to her Christian doctor, who very shortly committed Jesse to the hospital.

By seven-thirty that night convulsions had set in. The doctor called his wife and asked her to begin praying for Jesse. He broke the news to Judy that the diagnosis was meningitis, a very serious and often fatal disease, particularly in infants. By midnight Jesse had been rushed by helicopter to the intensive care unit in a Miami hospital.

And that is really about all we knew for three days.

Now when something like this hits you, all the game-playing stops. What you believe, what you have risked everything on, is either true or it's phony. Prayer is either a real, heart-to-heart communication with God, or else it is all a daily recital of superstitious ritual. Intercessory prayer, the prayers of friends and loved ones, is either a group exercise arising out of desperation to provide some kind of personal rabbit's foot, or else it is a real release of compassionate love flowing from the heart of God as a response to the giving of pure love and concern.

That first long night I fell apart. At that point I was miles from circumstantial happiness. Then I turned to the Word of God, began to shade my spiritual eyes and peer down into the darkness of the deep well within, and after a while *I saw the Living Water.*

I have said that sometimes spiritual and circumstantial happiness are intertwined; that is, the emotional and the spiritual are provided with great blessing within the circumstance.

It happened to me then. I knew the Presence and I was baptized—indeed, drowned—in peace, blessed by the Holy Spirit through His ancient but timeless Word, spoken to my heart.

Here is what I read:

How beautiful upon the mountains
    are the feet of him
  who brings good tidings,
who publishes peace, who brings good
    tidings of good,
who publishes *salvation,*
    who says to Zion, "*Your God reigns*" (Is. 52:7,
    italics mine).

I must tell you that the word "salvation" used here and most everywhere in the Old Testament is quite different from its New Testament usage. In the Old Testament it means "wholeness," for Christ had not yet come to bring eternal salvation.

Now read the last two lines again, substituting the word "wholeness" for "salvation." You will see very clearly what I saw in the depths of my well; it was His assurance to me!

A couple of days ago another phone call brought the good news: temperature back to normal, again taking food, all tubes and other devices removed. Today came the news that brain scans show no damage and Jesse will be coming home right away! They are calling him their "miracle child."

Today is a day when circumstantial and spiritual

happiness are combined. Today is a day for Cloud Nine! About the only thing you can call it when circumstantial joins with spiritual happiness is pure joy!

But what if Jesse had died?

Well, circumstantial happiness would have flown out the window, to be replaced with deep circumstantial sorrow. But I have been on that end, too, and I submit to you that spiritual happiness would have remained. Like Paul, we know that nothing "will be able to separate us from the love of God in Christ Jesus our Lord" (see Rom. 8:35-39).

If you are a child of God who walks with Him, the knowledge of that should be enough to cause all the hallelujahs you ever knew to join hands and dance around the cockles of your heart! And that, amidst your tears!

But I praise God for times of circumstantial happiness. If there were no such thing as a sudden, inexplicable upsurge of inward delight some frosty autumn morning as you walk along and observe how God's angel artists have painted the hills with a thousand colors, what would be the use of it all?

If there were no inward happy moments evoked by the smell of fresh bread, the sight of southbound geese trumpeting in the sky, the sight of little arms outstretched as your child greets you; if there were never emotions evoked by the tender, intimate touch of the beloved, the whispered assurances of love, the poignant fragile moment when a cherished dream has come true, then we would have been cheated in being born, and life itself would be a fraud imposed upon us without our consent.

But these are blessings God has provided for *everybody* in the world to enjoy from time to time.

In no way am I putting down emotions; both kinds of happiness obviously touch them. Nothing spectacular ever happens in a church that always must be dignified, nor in a person who must always be reserved due to some kind of inward psychological block. It is a necessity to express emotion, for we are made to function smoothly by doing so.

We used to have "memory verses" in Sunday school. We were supposed to commit at least one verse of Scripture to memory during the week and then recite it on Sunday morning in class.

Sometimes, though, when boyhood became too busy for memorization, I would fall back on that old reliable verse: "Jesus wept" (John 11:35).

But I know something now I did not know then — that this is one of the deepest, most profound verses in the entire Bible. Most people form a quick mental picture of Jesus just sort of dabbing at His eyes in a restrained sort of way.

But the Greek word translated "wept" here is *dakruo*, and it means "to shake silently with sobs." When He approached the beloved Holy City, Jerusalem, the Word says, "he beheld the city, and wept over it" (Luke 19:41, KJV).

The Greek word for "wept" here is *klaio*, closely akin to *dakruo*, meaning "to sob — to wail aloud." Our Lord Jesus was illustrating to us that emotions are a part of us, and that it is *all right* to express them. Standing there before that ancient city that had rejected Him, He "let it all out."

And woe unto the person who stifles natural emotions within for one reason or another, for that person is headed for trouble.

So I do not want you to get the idea that *only* spiritual happiness is important. Emotional happiness (or sorrow) is also vitally important. But the difference is simply that circumstantial happiness is a frothy thing. It does not last. It is like a lovely soap bubble blown by a child. Ascending upward, it somehow catches all the startling colors of the rainbow and traps them for a brief moment. Then it is gone.

Once at the close of a grand week of inspirational meetings, all of us were transported to the very heights of emotional happiness. The Lord indeed came upon us much like He did those on the Mount of Transfiguration. The light was dazzling. A dear woman with shining eyes clutched my hand and said, "Oh, Arnold, how can we keep this going? Tell us how we can keep on like this!"

"You can't," I answered. "This glorious moment will go away, although we will all be the richer for it. You can live on a higher plane than you did before, but you cannot keep this moment as it is. You can be more deeply committed than you ever have been in your life, but you cannot remain in this state of happiness."

To tell her otherwise would have been dishonest, and it would have laid the groundwork for future depression and false guilt.

But spiritual happiness abides because the Holy Spirit abides. There is no way He is ever going to leave us, not in the midst of shipwreck, beatings, stonings, or meningitis. The Holy Spirit abides—

you can count on it. Anytime you seriously care to lean over the well of your circumstances and peer down into the seemingly bottomless darkness, if you shut out the world long enough you will see the Water. You will be made not just a coper but an overcomer. Spiritual happiness comes out a trillion miles ahead of the circumstantial kind, that's for sure.

A man approached the captain of a whaling ship in the 1800s at Boston harbor. The captain was taking on crewmen for the voyage. He discovered that the man had never been on a whaler before, and he asked the man, "How can you expect me to hire a novice like you and take you out there with me where there are mountainous waves and terrible storms? Do you know anything at all about sailing?"

"No, sir, I don't," said the man. "But I know how to bail water when the ship is sinking!"

The captain gave him the job.

Spiritual happiness will teach you how to bail water when your ship is sinking. When circumstantial happiness vanishes, spiritual happiness keeps you going.

Like the young woman who sat in my office, maybe you have been seeking the wrong thing. Perhaps you were happy all along and didn't know it because you were confused about what true happiness is. Maybe you have allowed your circumstances to distract you from what you have seen in the well.

We were born into an unhappy world, and we need to know how to be happy in it, for if we don't we will waste this experience we call life.

We know that because of the very nature of existence there will be many more storms ahead, and that we have much to learn about dealing with them. I invite you to come along with me and together let's seek some answers. But we will not be going alone, for the Holy Spirit—the River within us — will go along.

And He will teach us how to bail.

2

What Do I Do
When Life Falls Apart?

It was about nine-thirty in the evening, a few
months ago. Martha and I sat in the family room of
our home on Faith Mountain. We had been sitting on
the porch swing outside, looking out across the
peaceful scene in Shoal Creek Valley as the evening
angels gently nudged the reddened sun down below
the horizon and tucked it in for the night.

We had come in and turned on the television set,
and had just settled back when suddenly a rough,
masculine voice said, "If you sit still and do what we
tell you, you won't get hurt!"

Startled, we looked around and saw two men,
nylon stockings over their faces, each holding a
handgun, one pointed at Martha and one at me.
They forced us to lie on the floor and bound our
hands and feet with nylon hosiery. One of them sat
in a chair, his gun pointed at us, while his companion
took about an hour to go through our house and take
the articles he wanted.

We lay there, not knowing if they would club us

with their guns, take our lives, or do things even worse.

Where moments before there had been a calm, placid time on the circumstantial waters of our lives, now there was a raging storm.

It seemed like eternity, but after about an hour the storm subsided almost as quickly as it had arisen. When the intruders had filled their sacks with the articles they wanted, they left us shaken but unharmed.

We had been bound loosely, so it did not take us long to work free and call the police. (Two weeks later one of the men was killed in an armed robbery, and the other was captured and is now in prison.)

After the officers left, Martha and I discussed our feelings. We were amazed at the deep inner peace that was given to us during this experience. I would have expected pounding hearts, an adrenalin flow, perhaps fear. But none of these things came into us. We had lifted our silent prayers and looked deep into the well, and *had seen the River!* It is the only way I know to explain the calmness and peace we had within.

So you can see that spiritual happiness does not depend on our problems or our circumstances. Circumstances are the mushrooms that grow up overnight in the forest of life. Quickly they come and go, and as they go others arise. It is all constantly changing. Any kind of safety pattern that we establish soon is blasted by the intrusion of threatening circumstances.

I am not trying to dismiss circumstances lightly.

They are real, and I know there are people reading these pages whose lives are filled with pain, tragedy, sorrow, anguish of soul, and threatening possibilities so unbelievable that no novelist would ever risk his credibility by setting them down in fictional form.

I know that, because I know what kind of an unhappy world this is.

But I know something else, and that is that this thing I am writing about is not something that springs up in the morning and is withered by night. I know that the deep serenity that comes from a knowledge of the abiding Spirit of God within is not transient. It is there in *every* circumstance because *He* is there.

The apostle Paul knew that, too. And here is what he had to say about this very thing:

> We are afflicted in every way, but not crushed; perplexed, but not driven to despair; persecuted, but not forsaken; struck down, but not destroyed (2 Cor. 4:8,9).

You think he didn't have the right to say that?

See him there in that dark, filthy, vermin-filled jail at Philippi. His back is so sore from beatings he cannot lean against the rough, scaly wall. The serum from his wounds runs slowly down his back into his breechcloth. His head aches, his tongue is thick and parched, and every muscle in his body screams with pain as the chains hold him spread-eagled against the wall. Blood is caked on the backs of his legs, and

33

nausea from shock is weaving in his stomach. He and his companion Silas have been there for hours, and now it is midnight.

He looks down at Silas, who is chained to the floor, and whispers hoarsely, "Silas — let's *sing!*"

Sing? Under these hopeless circumstances? What's the matter with you, Paul? Don't you know that now is the time to fret, stew, and worry? Now is the time to paint lurid pictures in your imagination about more whippings, stonings, or even the executioner's sword!

Don't you know that now is the time to get angry with God and open the door of your heart to an inrush of doubts about what you have believed, to ask all kinds of senseless, unanswerable questions? Questions like, "Lord, how could You let this happen to me? I've *tried* the best I know to serve You and be Your child, and now this! What is it with You, God? What's going on?"

Do you know the feeling?

But Paul doesn't heed those thoughts. He knows they are fire bombs straight from the enemy's cannons. Furthermore, he knows the proper antidote. He probably has just taken a long deep-well look and has seen the River, and he is able to say, "Let's sing."

Now is the time to praise God. Now is the time to plug in the cassette that has the Hallelujah Chorus on it. Now is the time to give thanks because of what you saw down in the well. So Paul says, "Brother, let's sing!"

You can read the whole story there in the sixteenth chapter of Acts, how Paul and Silas sang at midnight and the River flowing in them flooded its banks. The power of the Lord was released in that prison, and the walls fell down. And that night the jailer and his family found salvation in Jesus Christ.

If you love God deeply and abide in His Word, that's what will happen when life falls apart. When your circumstances become the most unbearable is when the depositories of Christian happiness are the fullest, and you can draw the cash of victory from them and spend it with reckless abandon, if only you will.

Hey, what is this—some kind of spiritual locker-room pep talk you're giving me? Is this some kind of escapist logic designed to help me forget my troubles? Are you setting me up for some kind of sky-high religious trip that will separate me from reality for a while?

No, I wouldn't do that to you even if I could. I am simply trying to show you that we are children of a God who *specializes* in making us more than adequate. He is the divine Sculptor who can chisel beautiful things from the hardest and ugliest rock you can hand Him.

That is what He did at Calvary. He walked straight up to the worst circumstance that could possibly happen to Him—the Cross—and turned it into the best thing that ever happened to all of us! And when you can do *that* you have a right to promise people that they can become "more than conquerors" (Rom. 8:37).

Some of the happiest people I have ever known

have been those with the most problems. And some of the most miserable people I have ever known have been those with the fewest.

Spiritual happiness simply *does not* depend on whether or not you got the new car, or if Junior graduated from college, or if you're short or tall, rich or poor, or if you got a traffic ticket; it is completely unrelated to your wardrobe, your checkbook, your crowded calendar, your diet, or whether or not your husband forgot your anniversary.

Anyone can know it in their deepest hearts—the shy people of this world or the clowns who go through life hiding their hurt behind their masks.

You could not very well say that Jesus died in circumstantial happiness, but you could indeed say that He died in *spiritual serenity*. Never did a more serene exclamation fall from anyone's lips than when in His very last breath He gasped, "It is finished" (John 19:30). It was an expression of spiritual happiness of the most profound kind.

Now, let me snuggle up to where you really are right now in your life. Could you stop this very moment, right where you are standing knee deep in the midst of your own big stack of frustrating circumstances, pause for a long moment and perhaps whisper, "The LORD is my shepherd, I shall not want," and take a long, deep-well look down into whatever darkness surrounds you? Do you see the River? It may be a faint reflection, but does it shines back up at you out of your darkness? Is it there? Is *He* there?

Of course He is, but do you know it for certain? I'm not talking about any kind of feeling. I'm asking, do you know it in the only way that any human can ever know — *by faith*?

If you are far enough along the Christian journey that you can answer, "Yes, I know it," then you are the possessor of spiritual happiness. And that ought to send a firestorm of rejoicing into your soggy spirit. That ought to turn up your furnace to the point where love and gratitude well up within you and serve you a little taste of Cloud Nine!

But what if you honestly looked and did not see the River? Well, we are going to deal with that in the very next chapter, but for now I want to give you a bit of added good news.

Sometimes the River appears unexpectedly when you need Him most. Sometimes the Holy Spirit of spiritual happiness bursts onto the stage of your life when you have given no cue for Him to enter.

Jesus experienced this in the Garden of Gethsemane. Let's review the scene together.

I think we seldom catch the sheer horror of Gethsemane. For years I thought of the old familiar picture of Jesus kneeling by the rock in the moonlight, a beam of light shining on Him and the dark trees outlined in the background. His peaceful face and deep-set eyes are focused toward the sky. No doubt a warm spring breeze is blowing. It is a rather tranquil scene. Funeral homes all over the country used to distribute hand fans with this picture imprinted upon them.

But in my opinion, this picture does not portray what happened in the Garden. Let me try to set down in a few paragraphs something that will at least give us a faint echo of the agony there.

The Scriptures say, "He ... began to be greatly distressed and troubled" (Mark 14:33). His heart was breaking. He was absolutely crushed and decimated. He began to wrestle over "the cup."

This cup He was about to drink—the cup of sin, sickness and death—was the spiritual hemlock that did Him in.

The Scriptures say, "For our sake he made him to be sin who knew no sin" (2 Cor. 5:21). In Monday-morning terms, Jesus was saying, in effect, "Now, Father, I open up My own life, My psyche, and take in the sin of the world."

In Gethsemane He became willing to put up all His antennae and receive into Himself the collective sin of every person since Adam—all the foulness, the filth, the degradation. It is a wonder to me that He did not go crazy right on the spot, as He comprehended what the Father was asking.

He was not kneeling nobly, with placid features and tranquil brow in the moonlight by a rock. *He was dying of poison,* and one who dies of poison does not die easily.

Isaiah says that on the cross Jesus was bearing all of the weapons from hell—not only sin, but also our sorrows and sickness (see Is. 53). All the cancer, the foul smells of osteomyelitis, all the blocked coronary arteries, the tuberculosis, the arthritis, the plagues —He was bearing all the pathological weapons of Satan. Yes, He was bearing death itself, for death is Satan's weapon, not God's.

See Him in your mind. Perhaps he was on the ground, contemplating all of this, writhing in awful cramping and pain, kicking His legs, groaning in agony, clawing at the dirt with His fingers until they were raw and bleeding. Some say Satan was trying to kill Him here before He could die on the cross.

This is something of what it was like to take into His soul all the wars, the killing, the perversion, all the lust that parades through our minds, the blasphemous oaths, all those ego trips of self-satiety. He was carrying it all, drinking into His divine personhood all of it, every last drop.

And then the Word of God says a wonderful thing. As Jesus was comprehending fully what lay just ahead, "There appeared to him an angel from heaven, strengthening him" (Luke 22:43).

Isn't that just like the Father?

After that, our Lord Jesus was able to arise and go on. He was made adequate for the Cross, and He met the arresters in complete serenity. The River of God rose up into His humanity, and He died with mercy on His lips and forgiveness in His heart.

No person on this earth will ever have impossible circumstances piled as high about them as did Jesus Christ on that dark night long ago. But the marvel is that God still functions in our helpless dilemmas precisely as He did that night. The strengthening angel still comes unexpectedly into our despair.

Do I just *believe* this, or is it something I *know*? Let me tell you what God did for us in the midst of our robbery situation. One of the burglars was sitting in my platform rocker, and Martha and I were bound and helpless on the floor. We had no idea what was coming—maybe death or, for her, even worse.

Then I noticed a very strange thing. Where was the pounding heartbeat, the throbbing temples, the sudden adrenalin flow in preparation for possible combat? Where was the white-hot heat of fear in the pit of my stomach? Where was the inner trembling?

None of these things was present. Instead, there came upon me a supernatural calm that was almost a complete inner *peace*. As I looked at Martha I was able to smile in assurance at her, and she was able to return a faint smile to me.

Then God did a spectacular thing; He wired together two little synapses in my brain and pressed the button on my computer, and *precisely* the right verse from His Holy Word was projected onto the screen of my mind: "Do not fear those who kill the body but cannot kill the soul" (Matt. 10:28). As it printed out, I *knew* that the River had swelled up out of the darkness and overflowed and *drowned* me in serenity. I was blessed of God. The strengthening angel had come!

After that, it did not matter what they did; all that mattered was that I knew Jesus was Lord of the situation.

It so happened that when the two robbers had finished taking what they wanted, they left without harming a hair of our heads. And as if the assurance God had given us in the middle of that experience was not enough, after the police had gone I opened the Bible to the Book of Psalms and Psalm 124 fell into my consciousness. God lit up the skies of my mind, set that psalm on fire, and let it burn its way into the awareness centers of my being until I *knew* He had spoken again in affirmation. Here are a few lines:

If it had not been the LORD who was on our side, when men rose up against us . . . over us would have gone the raging waters. Blessed be the LORD, who has not given us as prey to their teeth! We have escaped! . . . Our help is in the name of the LORD . . . (Ps. 124:2, 5-8).

He seemed to be saying, "In case you begin to doubt that it was I who gave you the inner assurance you needed, here is another affirmation just to make doubly sure you get the message!"

Dear friend, the gift of the Holy Spirit—the author of spiritual happiness, serenity, deep joy—is the way-down treasure that always lies glistening within us when we take the deep-well look. And sometimes, when we need Him most is just when He comes to us in ways that even the most skeptical person could never doubt.

So when life falls apart, He is always there to put the pieces back together again, if only we will hand them to Him!

3

If I Don't Have It,
How Can I Find It?

I have noticed a strange thing about wells. If you put a lid on them, you cannot draw water out of them!

Perhaps by this point you have begun to be a bit troubled, and you're thinking, "What's wrong here? I have been a Christian for a long time, but I really never have experienced anything like what is being described. At least, if I did it was a long time ago. When I look down into my well, there's nothing there!"

Maybe, just maybe, it's because there is a lid on your well! People who cannot relate to the "water-well promise" of Jesus (see John 4:14), who never know this deep serenity, this inward assurance, this spiritual happiness, may be certain of one of two things: either they have somehow put a lid on their wells, or they never had a well within them in the first place.

What do I mean by "having a lid on your well"? I used to visit a man whose well was covered up. On the walls of every room in his house hung religious mottos, such as "God Bless Our Home" or "Christ Is the Head of This House." This man was most faithful in attendance at worship. His speech was clean and his conversation was spiritual. He loved to talk about the Bible and how he "believed every word in it."

Yet he seldom smiled, his features were harsh and stern, and his opinions were locked like prehistoric reptiles in the immovable icy depths of frozen certainty. He had all the answers.

Eventually I learned that thirty years previously he had become alienated from his only daughter, and had not spoken to her since. There was a lid on his well.

Sometimes the lid slides into place gradually, not from a single incident but over a period of years. Paul realized this when he asked the church at Galatia, "Having begun with the Spirit, are you now ending with the flesh?" (Gal. 3:3).

You see, a stream always flows toward the ocean. When it is diverted from its purpose, it turns into a swamp. Many people start out along their journey toward Christlikeness with great joy and enthusiasm. But somewhere along the way, they allow the enemy to begin making inroads into their convictions, and the lids begin to slide over their wells.

If there is any such thing as a carnal Christian, Chuck certainly was one. He was a funeral director in a rather large town. A hail-fellow-well-met sort of person, he was a leader in civic and community affairs — president of the local Rotary Club, Greens Committee chairman at the country club, a real "nice guy" about town. Everyone liked him.

His two daughters and his wife sang in the choir at their church, but Chuck only attended at Easter and Christmas. However, there came a time—as it does for everyone—when the dilemma and the person came together. Chuck had a heart attack, and for days he drifted between life and death. His pastor visited him faithfully and prayed with him two or three times a day during those critical hours.

Then the recovery began, and soon Chuck was able to have visitors. His pastor would come, and there would be friends from the Rotary Club there. Before his pastor left Chuck would always say, "Fellows, my pastor is going to have a word of prayer." And they would bow their heads before God.

When his recovery was complete, Chuck came back to worship and attended faithfully for two years. Then gradually he began to miss a Sunday here and a Sunday there. When summertime came, he went to his home on the lake on weekends and dropped out completely. That fall he did not return to regular worship.

When it came time for the wedding of one of his two daughters, his pastor performed the ceremony in the church amidst ornate and lavish decorations. Afterward, the pastor was delayed and was late arriving at the reception.

"I took the elevator to the top floor of the finest hotel in town and went to the ballroom. I opened the door on the wildest, most drunken scene I had witnessed in a long time. Chuck saw me and rushed over, obviously embarrassed, and said, 'Pastor, you don't want to stay here. You just go down to the restaurant and get anything you want and charge it to me.'"

Then my pastor friend said, "I went downstairs and out into the street with a saddened heart. The Inner Spirit brought that text to my mind, 'Having begun with the Holy Spirit, are you now ending with the flesh?'"

Chuck had slid a lid over his well.

If we look down into our wells and we see nothing, it just might be because there is something between us and our Lord.

At this point we need to make something absolutely clear. Many, many times people have come to me for counseling and confided, "My problem is, I have lost God!"

We do not lose God. When we are born anew, the Holy Spirit comes *to abide* in us. What people should really say is "I have lost *contact* with God!" That is much more accurate. Something has come between us; there is a wall, a barrier, a lid, and the eye-to-eye, face-to-face relationship we once had has been blocked.

There are all kinds of lids. In fact, there are so many that we will devote the next chapter entirely to describing some of the tricks the enemy uses in trying to steal our spiritual happiness from us.

But, now, what about those who say, "I *never* have experienced this deep-well assurance you've been talking about."

We are promised the deep-well look or the inner witness of the Spirit (see Rom. 8:15,16), so if the

River is not there we can only presume that the abiding Spirit was never there.

There are two categories of people of whom this could be said: first, those who have known the Lord only intellectually, and second, those who have never known Him at all.

I have known many, many people from this first group—dear, dear people who indulge in all the forms of discipleship but who are not truly committed disciples. They attend worship, sing in the choirs, serve as officers and teachers in the church, and participate in all the ongoing programs. They do all the right things. They say all the right words. They are always at the right place at the right time.

But inside they are sterile. It never occurs to them to witness; they have no hunger at all for the Word of God; their prayer lives, if it were known, are barren and fruitless. There is no joy or excitement in them. Why?

They have never said yes to God *personally.* You see, you really cannot say yes to an intellectual proposition. You cannot say yes to the biblical narrative of Jesus Christ. You can only say, "I believe it is true."

Is God an intellectual proposition? Or is He a person? Is He a grey blob of mystical ectoplasm flitting about from planet to planet, who somehow was here before creation took place and in ways we don't understand caused it all to be?

Or must we ascribe to Him intelligence, purpose, and functions? If so, then we must also ascribe to Him *personhood.* Surely He is not the same kind of a person we are, but He does have personhood even as we do.

Therefore, the only way anyone can ever *know* God is in a person-to-person relationship with Him. And that person who is God has promised us over and over in His Word that He will come and indwell us. Read Jeremiah 31:33 and note the personal touch from God that is promised.

> But this is the covenant which I will make with the house of Israel after those days, says the LORD: I will put my law within them, and I will write it upon their hearts; and I will be their God, and they shall be my people.

And hear these words that fell from the living lips of Jesus Christ Himself concerning the promise of the indwelling Spirit: "You know him [the Holy Spirit], for he dwells with you, and will be in you" (John 14:17).

The simple gospel is that God loved the world so much that He sent His Son here to die for our sins, and when we receive *Him* (not "it") by faith, His Holy Spirit comes and indwells us. He is *there*; He is the River within, and we can look down through the darkness and *know* that He is there. Salvation is ours.

But even beyond that, we are promised that we shall live with Him *forever*. What is His is ours. Eternal life is His, and He shares it with us. All His kingdom belongs to us, because we have personally taken what He has personally offered us.

Somewhere I heard the story of a rich man whose

48

wife died. Not long after that his only son was killed in an accident. As a result of this deep sorrow, a few months later the rich man himself died.

He left no will, but he did tell his attorney that his longtime beloved house servant should have first choice of anything in the house. A painting of the rich man's son hung over the fireplace mantel, and after looking over the great house the servant said to the attorney, "I want the painting—because I loved him."

When the attorney took the painting down, he noticed a note taped to the back. After reading it, he gave it to the servant with a smile, for the note read: "Whoever takes my son inherits my fortune!"

If we are to inherit the fortunes of our heavenly Father, we must take His Son.

But how do we do this?

A dear friend of ours was on a ship coming home on the last day of World War II, the day the Japanese surrendered. The battle had been long and wearisome, but now they were approaching home. Excitement gripped them, but as they came into San Francisco Bay a dense fog covered the entire area. Visibility was practically zero, and as they came into the bay their radio compass went out. (All ships were not radar-equipped then.)

They could not send a radio message since they were observing military silence. The captain was frantic and said to my friend, who was the signalman, "Somehow, get us some help ... get us a position."

My friend told me, "For perhaps the longest ten minutes of my life I peered through the fog. Then I spotted a faint blinking light. It was sending the letter A, which in international Morse code language means, 'May I send?' "

"I quickly grabbed my blinker light and sent the letter K, which means, 'Go ahead.' "

The light began to blink again, this time spelling out these wonderful words: "I—am—the—harbor-pilot. May—I—come—aboard?"

My friend sent back a joyous "yes," and the pilot came aboard and guided them safely home to a joyful reunion with their precious loved ones.

To say yes to God through Jesus Christ means to lay aside everything but our need and to listen to him as He says, "I am your Savior; can I come aboard?" Then, when we give Him our joyous yes and entrust to Him our deepest self, He will guide us safely home to all that He has prepared for us.

We cannot claim the precious promises of the Bible as intellectual propositions. We cannot make a promise ours simply by saying, "I believe that promise is true."

All of God's promises must be claimed through Jesus Christ, for God keeps His promises not simply to accommodate us, but also to glorify His Son. Paul had no trouble seeing that truth clearly. He wrote concerning Jesus: "All the promises of God find their Yes in him" (2 Cor. 1:20).

If we want the River in us, we must say yes to God through Jesus Christ, and that means a "dying out" of the self. I can only speak for myself, but I dare say you would agree with me that there is a once-and-for-allness and also an everydayness about the "dying out" of the self.

If I Don't Have It, How Can I Find It?

I gave all of my heart and life to Jesus Christ a long time ago, yet I find I must do it over and over again if my well is to remain lidless.

Some tribal people in Africa were converted, and shortly afterwards a runner brought an invitation from a neighboring chief to a big celebration where there would be ribald, drunken behavior.

They sent a message back by the runner: "We are sorry we cannot come, but we died last Tuesday!"

If spiritual happiness is not ours, it is either because we have been committed only to an intellectual proposition or because we have never made an initial profession of faith in Jesus Christ to Him personally. Happily, these are conditions that may be rectified any time our deepest hearts are ready.

Here now is just an added bit of frosting on the cake: If our wells are not closed off by lids, from time to time *God Himself drinks from them.*

What do I mean? Well, if it is true that there are some things God cannot do, by His own self-limitation, until He finds people who pray (and I believe that so strongly that I have written two books around this truth*), then that means that sometimes He must use our open wells.

Let me illustrate from my own life. The two men who came into our home and bound and robbed us were men of violence. We later learned they were escapees from the Oklahoma State Prison, serving thirty years for various crimes. The night after they robbed us, they robbed a motel in our town and

*You Can Pray As You Ought, Thomas Nelson Publishers, 1977.
How Much Faith Does It Take? Thomas Nelson Publishers, 1980.

severely beat a seventy-year-old desk clerk.

They left a trail of violence wherever they went, yet they did not harm us. Why did we escape without being harmed? I believe I know. I cannot prove it, but I praise God that I have been liberated from the necessity of proving everything I believe by the slide rule and litmus paper.

I believe we escaped violence because a friend of ours had the lid off her well and the Lord drank from it.

The robbery occurred on a Sunday night. The following Wednesday we received a letter from Evangeline Carry, a very dear, Spirit-filled Christian who lives far across the state from us. We love Evangeline and her husband, but we do not correspond regularly and only call one another perhaps once a year by phone.

With her permission I want to quote from that letter at length, for it is a testimony of faithful obedience.

Dear Christian Brother and Sister,

I will extol Thee, my God and king and bless Thy name forever and ever. Every day I will bless Thee.

Martha and Arnold, we are just fine, but do you need special prayer? The Lord brought me up in the middle of the night from a sound sleep about 10 days ago. He said "Pray for Martha and Arnold." Believe me, I have prayed.

This evening, the burden has appeared again—(with the instruction) "Pray." Well, I have prayed (we both have). I've tried to call you—you are in our prayers—it just seems to stay in my head and heart (pray for) Martha and Arnold.

I've served God too many years not to follow this voice. Whatever is apparent out there, *you will come through,* God has promised me, I have the inner assurance.

Love,
Evangeline

And of course the date showed she was writing the letter on the very evening we were being robbed!

The lid was off her well, the River in her was flowing, and the Lord came and used the obedience of His child to bring protection and safety to us. How do I know this? Those of you who know *Him* would never ask this question, for within yourselves you already know the answer.

So if you have never said yes to God through Jesus Christ as a person, a power, and a living, dynamic presence, you need to do that, so the River of water He promised may begin to flow in you.

Besides, who knows when, for His own purposes, He might want to drink from it!

4

Tricks the Enemy Uses Trying to Steal It

Trying to walk away from the River within you is like trying to walk away from your feet.

When the Holy Spirit comes to indwell us, He comes to abide. He doesn't say, "Well, I've been with you for a year now. I believe I'll take a couple of weeks off." Neither does He say, "I've been with you all day long. You're going to sleep now, so I'll just go run a few errands of my own and I'll see you in the morning!"

No way. When the well is dug and the River is found, the installation is there to stay!

But we have seen that the well can be blocked. Your serenity, joy, and assurance can disappear under the lid.

And if there is any one thing the enemy wants to do, it is to steal your spiritual happiness away. His delight is in seeing you uptight, anxious, and tied in knots with fretting and worry. He is glad indeed when you are having a "dry spell" (when you are blocked off from your River).

And his bag is full of tricks of all kinds designed to

steal your spiritual happiness. He has all sizes, shapes, and descriptions — tailor-made for your particular personality, weakness, and circumstances.

His hand is quick to reach in and draw out just the right one. He simply cannot bear to see you filled with happiness and growing in the knowledge of the Lord. He is on the job.

This very week I met a dear Christian friend whom I had not seen in some time. "What have you been doing this summer?" I asked her.

Quick as a flash she answered, "I've been fighting Satan mostly!"

I said, "Well, join the crowd! Haven't we all?"

It is a constant battle — no negotiations, no cease-fires, no détente. Don't ever think the enemy is going to fall back, leave you alone, and go pick on someone else instead.

But the good news is, of course, that in Christ we are not Satan's victims. Rather, we are victors over him. We are no longer mere copers but conquerors. The simple reason is that the issue of who is the mightiest — our God or the enemy — was decisively settled long ago out there on that lonely, windswept hill called Calvary. The enemy soon had to sign the surrender papers, once and for all.

But even though the issue was settled and "lo, his doom *is* sure," he still fights on in the arena of our free will and seeks to destroy our spiritual happiness. He knows this Scripture in his head, but he does not know it in his heart as we do. It is our battle cry as we take him on.

Little children, you are of God, and have overcome

them [evil spirits]; for he who is in you is greater than he who is in the world (1 John 4:4).

Now let's describe and examine some of the enemy's tricks. We won't be able to cover them all, but it will be helpful to shed light on a few of them.

1) He tries to get us to tempt God.

In spite of the fact that the Bible clearly states that God cannot be tempted (James 1:13), the enemy is constantly after us to try.

Read again the story of Ananias and his wife, Sapphira. Acts 5 tells how they sold some property and Ananias brought in the proceeds and laid the money at the apostles' feet. At that time the members of the infant church were sharing all of their worldly goods in order to survive.

But Peter discerned in his heart that Ananias had misrepresented the total and kept some for himself. And Peter said, "Ananias, why has Satan filled your heart to lie to the Holy Spirit? . . . You have not lied to men but to God" (Acts 5:3,4). When he heard this, Ananias fell dead.

In a few moments, Sapphira came in with the same story. Peter asked her, "How is it that you have agreed together to tempt the Spirit of the Lord?" (Acts 5:9). And when she heard what had happened to her husband, she too fell dead at their feet.

Well, I'm a little more than glad that's not the way God deals with people in the church today who try to tempt Him, aren't you?

A businessman who was a devout Christian told

me, "I had a chance to make this big deal. I could make a lot of money by just a few little maneuvers here and there, but some of those moves were on the shady side."

(Now when people begin to talk like that, beware! When they say, "It's not quite according to Hoyle," what they really mean is it's crooked! It's sinful.)

The man went on, "But I rationalized by saying that these chances don't come along very often. So I kind of pulled open a drawer and put Jesus in it for a while. I made the deal and made a lot of money quickly. Then, sometime later I went back and opened the drawer where I had placed Jesus, and He was gone!"

Now what he really meant was that the enemy had stolen his spiritual happiness. The deep serenity was no longer there. The inner assurance was out of his reach because he had tried to tempt God. Sin had become a lid on his well.

The cardinal appeal in this trick is always, "Surely just this one time won't hurt anything!" And so the rational lie builds up to the deed.

Or sometimes we say (if not verbally, then in our own thought-reasoning processes), "God is a God of mercy and it is His nature to forgive. He has forgiven me before, so He will do it again." This is highly dangerous stuff, for it directly tests God and is the basis of the sin of presumption.

It is sad, but there are people who get zapped with a great experience in the Lord, they are anointed, blessed with His gifts, and then go through their daily lives walking out of step with the Holy Spirit.

It is difficult for me to say this, but if such a course continues, these people eventually reach the point where they are ashamed of Christ, and the enemy has successfully wiped out all traces of spiritual happiness.

Let us beware of testing God's goodness and His grace.

2) He wants us to quench God's Spirit.

The Word of God is very specific about this trick. So that we do not misunderstand or underestimate its importance, the Scriptures say simply, "Do not quench the Spirit" (1 Thess. 5:19) — short, sweet, and to the point.

The price we pay is loss of spiritual happiness.

To quench something, of course, means to extinguish, to put out.

Surely there are no genuine Christians in the world who would do such a thing to God. Surely God's children would never try to repress or block out the voice of their loving Father.

But the Bible assumes we are in danger here, for it specifically tells the disciples of Jesus Christ not to quench the Spirit.

It would delight my heart if I could tell you, "Well, I certainly wouldn't do a thing like that." But I fear I'm in this struggle with the rest of you. We must all do battle against this trick.

The truth is that most all of us carry a little glass of spiritual water so that we can "quench the Spirit" if He begins to put a little pressure on us at a point where we'd rather not be pressed.

Perhaps He opens up an opportunity for us to

witness to someone, and we say, "Now, Lord, if you don't mind I'd like to pour a little water on this and maybe a little later on we can get together on it!"

Or He speaks to us about some particular appetite, telling us, "This is the way to go." We reply, "You're speaking a bit too strongly right now, and I'd just as soon be listening to something else." And we dash just a bit of water on it.

In most cases we probably don't do this consciously or deliberately. It's more likely that we drift into habits, wherein if the Spirit begins to open up opportunities for us to become something better, more fruitful, purer, loftier, more like the things of Christ, then we just get out the old water glass again!

We look around at the sins of other believers and rationalize: "That's the way they're living, and I respect them, so, Lord, can't You back down just a bit? I don't want to become the funny person in the crowd!"

We quench the Spirit—and that ultimately boils down to a half-surrendered disciple. This happiness-blocker is subtle and seemingly innocuous. It doesn't seem like a world-shattering thing to quench God's words to us about some private area of our lives that really doesn't amount to much after all. Or does it?

Somewhere I heard the story of a farmer who had a strange sense of justice. He captured an owl that had been killing his chickens, and he tied half a stick of dynamite to its leg. He lit the fuse and turned the owl loose, expecting it to fly away and be destroyed in midair. But instead it flew into the farmer's barn, and the fire that resulted from the explosion burned the barn down.

That is precisely how our half-surrendered selves come back and wreck us when we toy with the enemy instead of putting him away. It is a serious thing to quench the Spirit of God, and when we do it our spiritual happiness, our deep serenity of assurance, fades away.

3) He tempts us to feast upon unworthy fantasies.

For years I carried around loads of false guilts because of unchristian or unworthy thoughts that kept parading through my mind. They still pop in now and then, but I have been delivered from carrying that needless load.

Once at a great gathering, after I had spoken on the power of God to deliver us from evil, a handsome young man in his mid-twenties asked if he could speak privately with me for a moment. We stepped aside, and a torrent of anguish poured from him.

"I want to be a completely surrendered follower of Jesus Christ," he said. "Time and time again I have surrendered my life totally to His lordship, yet I keep having these unChristlike fantasies. They just keep coming every day. What can I do? It seems to me if I were really surrendered I wouldn't have these kinds of thoughts."

I told him several things he could do to improve the situation, such as filling his mind so completely with the Word of God that there wouldn't be room for much else.

But he seemed to experience immediate relief when I shared that I had had the same problem once, and that no one could possibly feel more guilty than I had felt, or be more miserable than I had been. But one day the blessed Spirit had said to me, "I do not place blame on you for that over which you have no control."

I told the young man how then I had realized that there is no way we can stop unbidden thoughts from leaping into our minds. A just and loving God does not hold us responsible for them. We are never guilty of that which is beyond our control.

But at that point we have a choice. Although we cannot stop these thoughts from *appearing* in our minds, we *do* have a choice as to whether or not we feed and nurture and add to them! If we do that, then we enter the realm of accountability.

If the enemy can introduce an evil or unworthy thought and persuade us to dwell on, inflame, and inflate that thought, then he has found a way to block out our spiritual happiness. It is one of his oldest and most successful tricks.

4) He encourages us to harbor a critical spirit.

Criticizing the performance of other people is almost always a sign that there is something we know about ourselves that needs to be masked over. Think of that one among your friends who always has good things to say about people, and you will agree that that person has a pretty good self-image.

The Lord Jesus had a marvelous insight about this truth, and He admonished us with these words:

Why do you see the speck that is in your brother's eye, but do not notice the log that is in your own eye? Or how can you say to your brother, "Let me take the speck out of your eye," when there is the log in your own eye? You hypocrite, first take the log out of your own eye, and then you will see clearly to take the speck out of your brother's eye (Matt. 7:3-5).

Among my aquaintances when I was in my thirties was a man I simply did not like. To be honest, that is an understatement. The truth is I couldn't stand him. At that time I never quite could put my finger on the reason for my feelings.

He had a rich, smooth voice and was always pleasant and outgoing. He was tall, muscular, and extremely handsome. His skin was clear and deeply tanned, and his hair was thick and wavy. He was always immaculately dressed and was the very picture of confidence and self-assurance. It was disgusting! I couldn't stand him!

Consequently, on a few occasions I said things about him that were not complimentary at all. In fact, they were much less than that.

I did not know then why he "rubbed me the wrong way," but now I'm pretty sure it's because I saw in him all the social graces and physical attributes that I coveted but felt I did not have. I reacted with criticism, for I saw him as a threat. I'm happy to say that I came to love him, and have long since been forgiven for my attitude toward him.

Thus, when criticism of others becomes a part of our conversational lifestyle, spiritual happiness is stolen away by the enemy. The serenity is gone, the lid covers the well, and our Christian walk is punctuated by erratic "ups and downs," for we walk only in half-light.

5) He tempts us to pursue false illusions.

In 1942 the outlook was glum for the United States. The Japanese had virtually destroyed our fleet, except for our carriers, and were sweeping through the Third World unchecked. The morale of our people was at an all-time low. Then came the startling news that American planes had bombed Tokyo.

The news electrified this country. Hope surged through it. If our planes could still bomb the enemy's capital, perhaps all was not lost. But how had they been able to do it? We had no bases near enough; these were short-range bombers, B-25s. When reporters asked President Roosevelt where the planes had come from, he smiled and answered, "They came from Shangri-la."

Of course, they came from an aircraft carrier somewhere in the Pacific, but most people back then knew that he was referring to the city made famous in James Hilton's great novel *Lost Horizon*. Shangri-la was the lost city somewhere on this earth where all was peace, joy, happiness, contentment, and wisdom; where love and kindness reigned and war and hatred were no more; where prosperity and plenty flowed for everyone.

The story is about one man's search for the lost city. In the book he finds it. But in real life, people everywhere are still looking for their own Shangri-las. They never find them, for they are pursuing illusions.

The Word of God knows about Shangri-la. Proverbs 23:5 says, "Wilt thou set thine eyes upon that which is not?" (KJV). The Revised Standard Version states it like this: "When your eyes light upon it, it is gone."

There are so many illusions the enemy tempts people to spend their lives pursuing, and they all steal away Christian happiness and serenity. The next two tricks we will discuss are examples of illusions the enemy would like us to believe.

6) The ultimate reality is material.

Any eighth-grade science student ought to be able to see that this is a devil's lie, straight out of hell itself. Science has demonstrated this to us in an indisputable manner.

If we examine a living cell through the eyes of science, we see that it is composed of molecules. If we break these apart we discover that molecules are made of atoms, and if we split the atoms we discover that they are composed of tiny bits of electromagnetic energy called neutrons, protons, and electrons.

These tiny bits are nonmaterial; they are *energetic.* One of the most exciting days of my life was when I traced the word "energy" back to its roots and found that its root derivative means "*of a spirit.*" Thus, the ultimate reality is not material but spiritual!

When you take any form of matter apart like this, you discover basically that all matter is made of atoms. Imagine the process reversed and you see the method by which God created everything. He simply willed it, and out of His spiritual being there issued forth His own energy in the form of atoms with which He built everything that is.

So the ultimate reality is spiritual, and yet millions of people — many of them God's people — base their lives on the illusion that the basic reality is material. They knock themselves out as they focus their life-drives on the accumulation of things. That striving climbs to the number-one rating among their priorities until these goals unseat God from the throne of their lives, and they attempt to relegate Him to a lesser position. Inevitably, then, life eventually turns to ashes — because it doesn't work that way! God will not consent to be number two, or six, or fifteen. He wants to be number one, not because He has a big ego but because He knows that's the only way He can bless us and help us to grow as He desires.

No one understood ultimate reality better than Jesus. In the wilderness of temptation the enemy said to Him, "You have done without food now for forty days, so before we proceed with our conversation, why don't You just use the talent and power within You to turn that stone into a fine loaf of bread and satisfy Yourself?"

But the Lord Jesus saw right through that old trick, and He answered, "It is written, 'Man shall not live by bread alone, but by every word that proceeds from the mouth of God'" (Matt. 4:4).

Notice that He did not say man should not live by bread, but by "bread alone"! Bread is necessary, but it is not all there is to life. It is not even primary; there is more, much more to life than bread. Jesus had His priorities straight.

Not only does falling for this trick block off Christian happiness, but it eventually ends in disillusionment and often tragedy.

A friend of mine took me driving about in the "high society" section of a great city in the Mid-South. We drove past the three-million-dollar homes, the estates with walls about them and guardhouses at the gate.

"These are the people who have it made," he said. "See that one? Well, that fellow blew out his brains a couple of years ago. And see that one? That man is president of one of the large motel chains in this country. He's got it made, except that his wife ran off with another man and now he's drinking himself to death."

As we drove on he pointed out another estate. "This one, too, has it made. He is at the top, president of one of the largest banks in the South, but his son is locked up in an asylum because drugs blew his mind, and his only daughter is wandering about with the street people somewhere in this land."

Their eyes were "set upon that which is not," and when they finally found their Shangri-la, they found it was like sand sifting through their fingers. They thought desirable material circumstances would produce lasting happiness.

These are the dramatic stories of the extreme, but in a lesser way many, many of God's people fall into this illusion and become obsessed with the idea that things are what ultimately matter. They believe the big-ad people who constantly seek to evangelize us into believing that *things* are the basis for happiness in this world.

But over against that stands the Word of Jesus Christ, who never once preached against people making a decent living and providing for their families, but who strictly and constantly warned against the dangers "mammon" holds for people. He stressed repeatedly that life is more than food and the body more than clothing (see Matt. 6:24,25).

If we ever find that depression or excessive anxiety has taken over our lives, and we try to look down into our wells to get hold of God and find we cannot reach Him, then one of the first things we may want to do is ask, "Are we following the illusion that the ultimate reality is material?"

If the answer is yes, there is always a second beginning!

7) He wants us always to believe that
people will perform up to our expectations.

This illusion is perhaps the most serious of the tricks the enemy has in his arsenal.

To attempt to establish relationships on this basis is to lay the groundwork for heartbreak. This illusion is the primary cause for hatred, ill will, resentment, anger, and even international war — for governments are made up of people, and they simply will not measure up to others' expectations.

On a person-to-person basis in our daily lives, allegations fly back and forth.

"He didn't do what he said he would!"

"She double-crossed me!"

"He doesn't do his part!"

"She is so stubborn!"

"I thought I could trust him!"

"She doesn't meet my need!"

On and on the accusations and counteraccusations flow, and like a great stench from the earth they arise to the nostrils of God. Believing that others will perform up to your expectations is a sure-fire well-blocker!

So alienations result, friendships are broken, and deep pus-pockets of resentment are formed. The divorce rate soars, leaving trails of misery and despair. Spiritual happiness is shattered, and lids slide over wells. The result is inner turmoil, which sometimes explodes into physical manifestations such as hypertension, ulcers, arthritis, and all kinds of inner horrors.

Asking another person to live up to your expectations is the cruelest, most unfair, most impossible demand one human can make of another. When we ask for performances that will satisfy our demands, we are asking something of other human beings that they simply cannot give. Churches are unfair to their ministers, and vice versa; husbands are unfair to their wives, and vice versa; employers are unfair to their employees; and on and on.

Suppose the Lord Jesus had written His own contract of expectations. "Now in order for Me to love them they must measure up to the following expectations I have for them:

1. They must never try to stone Me.

2. They must never lie about Me.
3. They must never betray Me and arrest Me falsely.
4. They must not mock Me, whip Me, or taunt Me.
5. They must never turn against Me, spit on Me, or humiliate Me.
6. Above all, they must never crucify Me.

"If they do any of these things, if they do not perform up to My expectations, I am through with them. I'm finished, and don't expect Me to love them, much less die for them!"

What if He had said that?

When they ultimately nailed the Son of God to a cross and dropped it with a sickening thud into its socket in the ground, the first cry that fell from His lips was not an accusation that they had failed Him, or a threat to divorce Himself from them. Instead, it was an anguished plea that His Father would forgive them!

He could do that because He is never distracted by what people *do*; He always remembers who they *are*! He constantly sees other people not through only human eyes, but through the eyes of God Himself.

There is a verse of Scripture that always moves me deeply when I see it:

When he saw the crowds, he had compassion for them, because they were harassed and helpless, like sheep without a shepherd (Matt. 9:36).

As a married man, I simply must not see my mate through my own eyes. I'll demand too much. Joined to Christ, I can choose to see Martha through His eyes. I won't be distracted by what she may say or do. I see her through His eyes, and thus see past her imperfections to her potential.

Who is that person just now who is bugging the life out of you? Who is that one at the office, at school, down the street (or even at home!), who simply is not performing up to your expectations, who may be crucifying you even though you are not at fault?

Well, if you can see them through the eyes of Jesus Christ, you have found a way you can forgive them.

But how can we see people through His eyes? By faith, you borrow His eyes in your circumstances. Live your life *incident by incident.* In fact, that is the only way we *can* live life.

In the next incident in your life when someone falls short of your expectations, ask simply, "Lord Jesus, loan me Your eyes for a while that I might see this person as You see him." I promise that you'll get a different look at that person and at the entire situation.

Is this some kind of mysticism? Hardly! Actually it is only applied reasoning. Are we not promised eyes to see and ears to hear? If He loved us enough to give His entire body on the cross to save our souls, will He not donate His eyes to us to do His will?

The only caution here is to be sure you look *long* enough! It may take a while for you to learn to see other people through Christ's eyes. You may have to wait until your emotions relax before you can focus. But if you look long enough, you will see.

And remember, people always need loving the most when they deserve it the least!

There is simply no end to the tricks of the enemy. However, they are all directed toward one thing —destroying your serenity, cheating and robbing you of the blessings of the Christian life.

Jesus knew how to handle the enemy. Several times when He was personally threatened with bodily harm, Scripture tells us He simply looked His enemies in the eyes and walked away, and they were rendered helpless.

One trip to his home town of Nazareth turned out to be a fiasco. The people asked Him to preach. They gave Him a great introduction and hung on to His every word. But then He began to step on their collective toes, and they couldn't stand the pain. They rose up and took Him to the city limits, where they meant to throw Him from a cliff. But the Word of God says: "But passing through the midst of them he went away" (Luke 4:30).

Satan has to have handles before he can grasp us. But Jesus was without sin, so the enemy had no handles to grasp. There are all kinds of handles —anger, fear, bitterness, jealousy, envy, covetousness, alienation, doubt. There is no end to the list, and the goal of the enemy is to trick us into giving him a handle.

You can keep your spiritual happiness by recognizing temptation before you yield. Learn to willfully check thoughts, fantasies, and critical attitudes the moment you see them coming. Develop a habit of saying no instantly to the enemy and to all his bogus offers.

5

When the Circumstantial and the Spiritual Clash

It is nine-thirty at night. You are the pilot of a Boeing 711 jetliner and you are bringing it in for a landing at Miami International Airport. There is a violent thunderstorm going on, the turbulence is severe, and torrential sheets of rain are pounding the runway. Visibility is practically zero and you are landing on instruments.

In your headset you are hearing two voices. One is that of the air-traffic controller, who has access to a vast amount of data and knowledge in the high electronic technology surrounding his desk. He is guiding you in. Your instruments confirm what he is saying to you.

The second voice is coming from your senses, from your sight and your sense of equilibrium. You peer through the blinding rain, straining to catch a glimpse of the runway lights. Your senses are telling you, "You're drifting to the left; pull her back. Your nose is too low; pull it up!"

But the voice from the tower is saying, "Steady

now, you're doing fine. Your flight path is perfect; just hold it there!"

The lives of two hundred and twenty passengers depend on your decision. Which voice will you trust? Will you trust your severely limited sight and your own sense of inner equilibrium? Or will you trust the voice from the tower, which has access to far greater wisdom and knowledge than you do?

Well, you had better trust the voice from the tower! The safety and well-being—and yes, the happiness—of all aboard depend upon your obedience to *that* voice, and not to your own.

We are in the "how-to" stage of our journey just now. We have covered what to do when life falls apart, as well as some of the major tricks the enemy uses in his attempts to slide lids over our spiritual wells.

Now we come to the question of what to do when the voices of circumstance are in direct conflict with the voice of our inner spirit. Remember that we are body, mind, and spirit (soul), and that the Holy Spirit communes with our spirits through our minds and emotions.

Sometimes what has filtered through our minds from the River directly contradicts the voices of our circumstances.

Let's go first to the Word of God for three such examples, and then to a present-day example.

Joshua had to fight more than just the battle of Jericho. He had to fight a battle within himself. Let me set the scene. The wilderness wandering had finally come to an end. Joshua had led the Israelite people down the valley of Gilead and they had

Inner Voice
Instincts
Reasoning

76

crossed the Jordan River into the Promised Land.

But dead ahead of them lay the first major obstacle — Jericho. It was a mighty fortress, set on rising ground at the foothills and highly defensible. The inhabitants had seen the Israelites coming from afar, and they had closed the mighty gates. The strong little army inside was ready.

But Joshua was the possessor of spiritual happiness. He and the Lord of Hosts had a face-to-face relationship. God had spoken to him many, many times, and He had just proven His support by parting the waters of the flooding Jordan so the Israelites could cross. Joshua *knew* the Lord was with him.

You can read the Lord's instructions in Joshua 6. In effect, this is what He said: "I didn't bring you this far to have you defeated. So you select seven priests and give them rams' horns, and you and all your men march around the city once a day for six days. On the seventh day, march around it, have the priests blow a mighty blast on their rams' horns, and tell the people to give a great shout.

"The walls will fall down and there will be such confusion and disorder that you will be able to go right in and take the city without a struggle!"

That is what the voice of the Lord told Joshua. But Joshua was a military man, reared in a military home and trained through the years in battle tactics and maneuvers.

Since Joshua was thoroughly human, it is highly probable that he heard another voice — the voice of his circumstances.

"Joshua, that has to be the most irrational, illogical set of instructions you ever heard. Line up your spearmen, deploy your bowmen, bring up your heaviest battering rams, be prepared to take severe casualties, and hit that city head-on! That's the way to deal with Jericho, or any other foe!"

We know which of the two voices Joshua obeyed, and we know that his obedience to God's voice brought about the desire of his heart — the downfall of Jericho.

I am saying that when our inner spirits tell us something that is in line with the Word of God, we had better obey *that voice* instead of the voices of our circumstances.

You could not wound me more deeply than to accuse me of being anti-intellectual, but I must say again that sometimes our minds insist on telling us things that directly contradict what we are receiving from our spirits and from the Word of God. When we obey the voice of our spirits and the Word, that is what the Bible calls *faith*.

That is how to keep the lid off your well. That is how to keep the knowledge of the River that flows within. That is how to maintain spiritual happiness.

Acts 27 tells how Paul was shipwrecked as the result of a terrible storm. He and the crew were washed ashore on the little island of Malta in the Mediterranean. The next chapter tells how the natives built a fire to warm the wet, shivering sailors. Paul gathered a bundle of sticks to feed the fire, but a poisonous viper crawled from the sticks and "fastened itself" on his hand.

Like Joshua, Paul was human even as we are, and the voice of his circumstances must have told him,

"Paul, you are a dead man! That viper is deadly poisonous, and no person can live after having been bitten by one!"

But Paul had heard another voice the night before. When the storm was at its worst, he had testified to the others aboard ship:

> This very night there stood by me an angel of the God to whom I belong and whom I worship, and he said, "Do not be afraid, Paul; you must stand before Caesar . . . . " So take heart, men, for I have faith in God that *it will be exactly as I have been told* (Acts 27:23-25, italics mine).

So Paul did not listen to what his mind must have told him out of his circumstances, for he had heard God's voice in his spirit, and he stood on that. There was no lid over his well on that chilly morning.

Again, when the voices out of the circumstantial begin to tell us something that conflicts with what we have heard from the River within, obedience to *that* voice—His voice—is the only way to spiritual happiness.

Let's look at one more example from the Scriptures. In Acts 12, Herod had Peter arrested and promised him that the very next day he would deliver him from the weight of his head. Yet Acts 12:6 says:

> The very night when Herod was about to bring him out, Peter was sleeping between two soldiers, bound with two chains.

What is wrong with you, Peter? How can you

sleep so peacefully between those two big burly soldiers when tomorrow you are going to die? Now is the time to storm heaven's gates with panic prayers and pleas for deliverance!

But Peter had heard another voice, and in my heart I know he remembered it then. The risen Lord Himself had told him:

> "When you are old, you will stretch out your hands, and another will gird you and carry you where you do not wish to go." (This he said to show by what death he was to glorify God.) (John 21:18,19).

Peter did not listen to what his mind was telling him through his circumstances, for he was not yet old. He had heard the Word of the Lord and he believed it, so he slept in peace.

I am saying that when we have heard from the Lord, and His Word contradicts what we can see, touch, taste, smell, or hear, faith trusts what we have heard. Faith does not *deny* the circumstances, but it trusts in God in spite of circumstances. Why? Because faith knows that anything sensory is subject to change, but what is spoken by the Lord surely endures and abides and cannot be changed!

That is "foolish" truth!

But all of this is not just truth for Bible times; it is steaming hot with freshness and relevance for our circumstances today. Kevin Lagree is a graduate of the Harvard Law School. A brilliant young lawyer, he joined one of the most prestigious law firms in Kansas City and was rising rapidly. His future was secured.

But Kevin and his wife, Patty, were born anew, and the Holy Spirit drilled a deep well within them and the River began to flow. The voice of the Lord told Kevin he was needed in the ministry of the church.

So in his mid-thirties, Kevin was led to give up his law career, enter theological seminary (where he graduated with high honors), and become the pastor of two little struggling rural churches in Kansas.

I counseled with Kevin a bit and I know something of the struggle that went on as the circumstantial and the spiritual clashed. The circumstantial voices said, "Kevin, have you lost your mind? You're young; you have the responsibility of a wife and two children; your future is assured. Man, you've got it made! Don't be a fool!"

But Kevin had heard another voice, too, and he obeyed that one. Needless to say, Kevin and his family were never happier than they are today. They have that peace, serenity, and spiritual happiness that can *only* come upon those who have said yes to the voice from within, when every outward evidence from the circumstantial seemed to indicate otherwise.

When we have *not* heard from the Lord and His Word has *not* spoken to us in our particular circumstances, then is the time to trust the best human logic and judgment with which He has blessed us, believing that He is on the job and will see us through. That, too, is faith — perhaps even a higher kind of faith, the kind that trusts the Father in the blackest midnight when there are no words from Him.

When the circumstantial clashes with the spiritual, and there has been a voice from the River, then is the time to cast your lot with Him. And in God's perfect timing the cup you have held out to Him will be filled.

6

How to Go to War
Against the Enemy

We live in a radically unhappy world. Several factors are responsible. First of all, there is the enemy. In the last chapter we discussed how he works on us individually. But the Bible also graphically describes how he works in the world:

> For we are not contending against flesh and blood, but against the principalities, against the powers, against the world rulers of this present darkness, against the spiritual hosts of wickedness in the heavenly places (Eph. 6:12).

This is no banana-republic rebel with a small band of part-time guerillas we are up against!

Secondly, in order to give you and me freedom of choice in this life, God has permitted evil a limited access to us. Sometimes it even seems that sin is on an equal basis with His access to us, and therein lies the battle for spiritual happiness.

We are God's children, but this does not mean we have received some kind of spiritual vaccination that renders our world immune from the assaults of the evil one. As Christians, we are assured that we "are all sons of light and sons of the day; we are not of the night or of darkness" (1 Thess. 5:5).

Even so, we are not placed in plastic bubbles to enjoy fellowship, share Christ, and grow without any outside interference from the adversary.

No, we are set free in an unhappy world of bondage. We have found spiritual happiness, but when we were born into the kingdom God did not remove our human flaws or our free wills. He simply gave us new hearts—a fresh set of righteous desires and godly motivations.

We must learn to live in that unhappy world and allow Him to lead the battle for us. And He will, for our Christ is not a sideline coach sending in instructions; He participates in the games with us, and that makes all the difference.

Some dear people get such a shot of spiritual adrenalin when they meet Jesus Christ that they ascend to emotional heights of bliss and innocently suppose that Christians are somehow taken out of the harsh environment of the world, to spend the rest of their lives smelling spiritual roses and eating chocolate-dipped cones of glory.

But the crash always comes, for the raw reality is that we must live within this unhappy world.

Precisely what kind of an unhappy world is this, in everyday shoe-leather terms?

There are power-hungry nations; the haves oppress the have-nots; greed is the chief motivator for the majority of national sin. Love has come to mean anything that provides sensory gratification between consenting adults; the new term is "recreational sex."

Every newspaper brings accounts of love-starved, sin-sick people who rob, steal, and murder; of men who beat their wives, batter little children, and torture, maim, cripple, and rape old people. There are people who sell drugs like candy to little children, and their minds are blown away. There are sex merchants who lure twelve-year-old girls into prostitution and who make pornographic movies using six-year-old kids. There is incest, adultery, embezzlement, and all the ugly rest.

This is the real, unhappy world where death lurks every hour of the day, as there are red buttons on the desks of world leaders that could initiate the destruction of civilization in half a day's time.

But glory to God, there is another side to it!

An old lady said to her pastor once, "God sure lets the devil have a lot of rope these days, doesn't He?"

Her pastor replied, "Yes, but He still keeps hold of the end of it Himself!"

That is the redeeming factor—that even in the midst of all the ugly squalor I have described (and I have scarcely scratched the surface!), our God is able to draw us up out of miry pits and give us a new song to sing in the midnight (see Psalm 40). He is not content to equip us with just enough to get by; we are empowered to be more than conquerors.

As victim, Christ canceled the penalty of our sin. But as victor, He trampled down death and hell and ransacked Satan's domain. And remember, it was God Himself who was nailed to that cross by the hosts of the enemy. When they had done Him in, they carried His body down the hill to a new tomb, which they closed with a great stone. On it they stamped in hot, new wax, the very seal of the emperor himself.

But in three days' time, God's eternal divine energy localized within that tomb and transmuted dead flesh to live tissue, bringing that dead corpse back to life. Our living, sovereign Savior arose! The earth was filled with the dynamic reality of a victorious Christ.

That same Lord walks in us through the tragedy-laden streets and alleys of this world today with saving and transforming power. Even as He was brought forth from death unto life, so people today are brought forth from spiritual death unto life (see 1 John 3:14).

He plucks people from Satan's hands; He rescues them from their senseless, illusory Shangri-las; He restores damaged marriages; He re-alters alternative lifestyles and gives people the victory. How? By giving us His Holy Spirit, who is Himself the River of Life within us, springing up into everlasting life.

He has done that in you and in me. Now we know the startling difference between mere circumstantial happiness and the deep-well kind, which we call spiritual happiness. We know the serenity that is far deeper than our emotions or circumstances, because we know the River and we know He is there. If we want to know how to be happy in an unhappy world, we must learn what life course to follow. And we must learn that from instructions from God's Word. We had better not go to war

against the enemy unless we have been thoroughly
briefed.

There is a great little chunk of condensed instruction in the sixth chapter of Ephesians concerning how to navigate in our unhappy world. You can lift it out and devour it as neatly as you lift out a piece of cherry pie with a spatula.

> Stand therefore, having girded your loins with truth, and having put on the breastplate of righteousness, and having shod your feet with the equipment of the gospel of peace; above all taking the shield of faith, with which you can quench all the flaming darts of the evil one. And take the helmet of salvation, and the sword of the Spirit, which is the word of God. Pray at all times in the Spirit, with all prayer and supplication (Eph. 6:14-18).

Now let's take the piece of pie and devour it, a bite at a time.

1) Loins girded with truth.

The overall picture here is of a soldier dressing for battle. The first garment he dons is the one next to his body, the closest to his person. That means that the underlayer of everything is bedrock truth.

What is truth? Truth in condensed form is nowhere better stated than in the words of Jesus, recorded in John 3:16:

> God so loved the world that he gave his only Son, that whoever believes in him should not perish but have eternal life.

It's that basic, although some folks try to make it very complex. But we begin here or we miss it all.

A letter came last week from a lady who is earnestly seeking God. In the process of trying to work through all her rational doubts, she wrote, "The only absolute in the creation is Einstein's theory of relativity."

In answering her letter I wrote, "My dear, I think you are wrong. There are many, many absolutes in the creation. The problem is that there are also many minds trying to define them. But the absolutes don't pay any attention to our definitions, for after we have finished with them the consequences just roll in anyhow."

I wished she could have known Claire Childress, who after she was reborn stood up to testify: "I just got tired of always trying to define God. I decided I'd never get anywhere until I met Him. Now I know you can never define God, but anyone can know Him."

The Bible says that "Jesus is Lord" (Rom. 10:9). All the magnificent, cosmic grandeur of the eternal Father Himself is, for us, reduced finally to those three words. If you want to keep your spiritual happiness in the midst of this unhappy world, gird your loins with *that*.

2) The breastplate of righteousness.

The breastplate protects the heart, which is also where the battle takes place. A bad self-image causes stress cracks to appear in the breastplate. Leviticus 19:18 tells us we are to "love your neighbor as yourself." It is difficult for those who don't love themselves to love other people or God.

The righteousness of Jesus Christ can take care of that. There is no one who knows that better than I. In my earlier years I was at times grossly overweight. Even when my body was satisfied by food, waves of compulsion would sweep over me from time to time in a demanding storm, and I would eat and eat and eat.

I could not understand it. I knew that gluttony is a sin and that I was morally responsible for it, but what was its basic cause in my case?

Gradually I came to realize that this compulsion sprang out of the fact that I was having problems loving myself. It was a compensatory symptom of something far deeper. I learned that my opinion of myself was the trigger. I knew my own sin-stained heart, and carried in my mind all the memories of past carnality and indulgences. I could not believe I was lovable to anyone — especially to God.

But one day God gave me a new heart, and when I became His my loving heavenly Father covered me and clothed my spiritual nakedness with the perfect righteousness of Jesus Christ. Now I could love myself, because I *knew* God loved me. When I finally got a long clear look at who Jesus Christ is, I discovered who I am.

It did not remove the damaging compulsions, but it transferred the burden of my past from my shoulders to His. I found that He could control my problems because He is Lord over them. In Christ I could love myself. I had put on the breastplate of (His) righteousness, and spiritual happiness was mine.

3) The shoes of the gospel.

When Paul wrote this phrase, he was probably thinking of Isaiah's statement: "How beautiful upon the mountains are the feet of him who brings good tidings" (Is. 52:7).

Paul is referring here to witnessing. We are commanded to be Christ's witnesses, and if we wish to keep our spiritual happiness we must obey. But immediately some will complain, "Oh, I could never do that. I'm too shy; it's just not my nature."

Sure you can. Anyone can. You don't think our Lord would ask us to do something without giving us the power to do it, do you? He promised us that power! "You shall receive power when the Holy Spirit has come upon you; and you shall be my witnesses" (Acts 1:8).

Well, the Holy Spirit *has* come upon you. He is the River within. In the next chapter we will discuss some creative helps for witnessing.

4) The shield of faith.

In our bedroom we have a well-known saying framed as a constant reminder that we have a sure defense against the enemy.

Fear knocked at the door. Faith answered, and no one was there.

The function of a shield in ancient days was to ward off arrows directed at you. When you saw the arrow coming, you held up the shield, which deflected it and bounced it harmlessly away. Paul calls these arrows "the flaming darts of the evil one."

American Indians used flaming arrows to set fire to pioneers' cabins. In a similar fashion, Satan constantly fires flaming missiles at us. His arm never tires; his supply of arrows seems endless. And he has all kinds in his arsenal—arrows of inferior feelings, fear, worry, fretting, anger, resentment, false guilt—you name them and he has them.

A recovered alcoholic told me, "When the drinking urge comes on me, I simply say to the devil, 'Go and pester God; I distinctly remember giving that habit to Him!' " He had the shield.

Black pastor E. V. Hill told in a sermon how one night he received a phone call informing him that the Ku Klux Klan was in his area. The rumor was that they were coming to burn his home. And he said, "I had the peace of God in my heart, and when you have that you don't have to worry and fret. So I went back to bed and went to sleep!" He had the shield.

Dear friends, the foe has no armor-piercing weapons for the shield of faith. This weapon, a gift from our blessed Lord, can help us stand against anything this unhappy, lost, and dying world can give us. Whatever your circumstance is right now, He is holding out that shield to you. Take it from Him, and you will find that your River is still flowing.

5) The helmet of salvation.

It is interesting to me that in this passage we are instructed to cover our heads. I understand that to mean we are to protect our minds from the enemy, for it is through the head that his missiles enter and work destruction to the entire spiritual body.

The helmet suggested is that of "salvation." This word means vastly more than being saved for heaven; we are not only saved *for* something, but *from* something. And one of those "somethings" is invasions of the mind by our foe.

His greatest technique is rationalization. If he can get us to do that, we are done for. The rationalizing of temptation means that we swallow a rational lie. Satan desperately tried to get Jesus to fall for this. In the wilderness he asked the famished Lord to turn stones into bread (see Matt. 4:3).

In the Bible, the word "bread" denotes a complete meal—sometimes a veritable banquet. Allow me now to do a bit of paraphrasing (quite a bit, as a matter of fact!).

Here were Jesus and Satan in the wilderness. The devil is a taunter as well as a tempter, so he said to the Lord, "Now, Jesus, you're hungry, aren't You? You've been up here a long time. You're in bad shape—in fact, You're right on the edge of malnutrition. Now, Jesus, use Your head. If You are God's Son . . . and I'm not at all sure You are . . . then Your Father loves You and doesn't want to see you hungry and hurting like this.

"So Jesus, just take those stones and say the word, and turn them into crisp, brown, fried chicken, some buttery mashed potatoes, white creamy gravy with little brown flecks of crust floating around in it, a slice or two of homemade bread, a cold soft drink with lots of ice, and a big slab of apple pie with a scoop of ice cream on it."

Then he laughed, "Wouldn't You like that? What kind of a heavenly Father wouldn't want You to have a meal like that?"

Jesus' head was spinning: He was weak and it sounded so enticing. But He said, "Oh, no, Satan, I'm not falling for that rational lie."

6) The sword of the Spirit (the Word of God).

Then Jesus put on His helmet and struck the enemy with the sword of the Spirit—the Word of God. He quoted Deuteronomy 8:3 when He said, "It is written, 'man shall not live by bread alone'" (Matt. 4:4).

Thus He overcame that temptation. You can read about it in Matthew 4. Further, our Lord used His sword to overcome every other rational lie the devil had for Him at that time.

John the revelator calls the Word of God a "sharp sword" (Rev. 19:15). So if we want to be happy in an unhappy world—if we want to be in it, walk through it, and stay on top of it in spiritual happiness and victory—it is vital that we, God's people, have this weapon at hand on instant-ready alert.

The Word must be hidden in our hearts, and the only way to do that is to feed from it. If we do not have the hunger for it, then we must prevail upon God to give it to us until the hunger comes.

A Christian without the Word in his heart is like a soldier without his weapon. The battlefield is far too dangerous to be out there without it.

7) Pray at all times.

A Christian without a vital prayer life is terribly handicapped. His spiritual happiness is a fleeting, wispy thing that he rarely knows. The lid is nearly always on his well, except perhaps during extreme crises.

But we seek a happiness that is constant, and we cannot have it unless we have a warm, personal, loving relationship with the Giver of happiness. How can we keep the lids off our wells if we do not know the River?

In one of Ionesco's plays a man and woman, two commuters, meet on the train to New York going to work. They ride together daily. In conversing, they discover they both live in the same apartment building and that they each have a daughter. Then they discover they are married to one another!

Strangers within a marriage!

Jesus Christ is the Bridegroom. The church is His bride. We are the church. How ironic it would be to ride through life together on a casual basis. If we want to know the exciting depths, the heights, and the joys of Christian happiness, if we want to grow in the breathless knowledge and revelation of who Jesus Christ is, then there must be developed that unique intimacy that only togetherness can bring. Prayer is that togetherness.

Thus, in that little exciting chunk of instruction from the Holy Word lies much of the secret of being happy in an unhappy world. To wear the armament of God is vital; the alternative is perishing. For the battle rages all about us.

If we are not equipped with it we are shot down by the unhappiness of the world, for we are constantly besieged and set upon. There are the daily newscasts with their heralds of doom and a steady stream of greed, tragedy, and crime. If we are not equipped we will be done in by political double-talk from governments, which ignore real needs and issues and are always seeking to preserve their own lives; by the constant negative intrusions of Dow-Jones averages, price indexes, and leading economic indicators.

We will surely succumb to the constant altar calls of the pied pipers of commerce, who smoothly tell us that their goods are the answer to those seeking happiness. When these goods are finally ours they turn back into pumpkins at midnight, and when morning comes they leave us in personal squalor and disillusionment.

But we are armed with the power of God Almighty. We have found spiritual happiness. We have looked down deep into the wells of our circumstances, and there we have found the Author of birth and life and death and everything else. We have found there the Mighty One who loves us with an everlasting love, a love that even when we can only catch a far-off glimpse of it leaves us breathless with joy and inspires and motivates us to want to know and experience more and more of it.

The fallout from that love creates a spiritual nuclear reaction within us that mushrooms up out of our wells and simply smothers us with serenity, and in our heart of hearts we are "happy in the Lord." There is no better way to say it than that.

Yes, we surely live in a Good Friday world—but we are Easter morning people!

7

The Secret of Spending
Beyond Your Means

Now that we know what spiritual happiness is, and
have received some admonitions and instructions in
waging spiritual warfare with the enemy and in
dealing with the clash between circumstantial and
spiritual voices, we need to go on to what I call some
"foolish truth."

This is truth that is so opposite from what the
world thinks that if you dropped it into the world's
computer a gigantic "reject" light would come on.

God's Word says in 1 Corinthians 1:27, "God chose
what is foolish in the world to shame the wise."
That's "foolish truth," and here are a couple of examples:

Whoever seeks to gain his life will lose it, but
whoever loses his life will preserve it (Luke 17:33).

Give, and it will be given to you; good measure,
pressed down, shaken together, running over (Luke
6:38).

Now that is "foolish truth." What makes sense to the world is, "If you want to save your life — protect yourself." Or, "Don't give it away. Keep it and pile it up for a rainy day. That's the way to have more."

We usually think of Luke 6:38 as referring to money, but its deepest meaning is far more inclusive. It is not just the Lord's financial counsel; it is the deepest law in the universe. If out of love we give anything away, we get back more.

One grain of wheat is planted in the earth and dies, but in dying it gives back something like one hundred and eighty wheat grains per stalk.

All this is to say that the greatest truth about spiritual happiness is simply that in order to keep it, you have to give it away!

When the River within (the Holy Spirit) prompts us to witness to others concerning Him, others are blessed and the water level in the River of life rises a bit within us.

When the Lord Jesus Christ drilled the well in your spirit, the inner River that resulted does not exist so that only *you* may drink from it. The well Water that "springs up into everlasting life" must be shared. Someone has said, "When your cup gets filled, splash on somebody!"

Witnessing involves a spending of the self. That is what Calvary is all about. Every river has to have an outlet in order to continue to exist. On the cross, the Lord Jesus spent Himself completely for the sake of the beloved, and the Father gave His life back to Him, as well as the lives of countless millions of others, including you and me.

98

The same principle applies to us. You and I are not called on to die on a cross, but to "die to self" in the spending of that self for the sake of others. That is why we *must* witness.

But when you mention the word "witness" to people, they panic. "I'm not the type!" "It's a special gift!" "I'm too shy!" "My faith is too private." Have you ever heard — or used — any of these protests?

Witnessing is not an option for Christians; it is our lifeblood. We either do it and grow, or we dry up.

If you are one who said you could never be a witness, what you probably meant was you can't fit into some kind of preconceived image you have concerning what a witness is.

Maybe you have a mental picture of a person standing on a busy street corner somewhere handing out tracts, or someone buttonholing people on airplanes, in supermarkets, or in the beauty shop to tell them about Jesus.

Well, that's what I call "cold-turkey" evangelism. God uses it, but not many people are proficient at this. The truth is that considerable harm is done by well-meaning but tactless people who do it poorly, or from questionable motives, such as trying to prove to themselves they love the Lord or to escape false guilt feelings that come if they don't.

I believe that a cardinal rule to remember is that we should *never* witness until the Holy Spirit within prompts and whispers "Now!" After all, *He* is the true witness, not we (see 1 John 5:7).

But anyone can witness, and thus keep spiritual happiness fresh and growing. The problem is that most of us want to do great, spectacular things for the Lord. It is difficult for us to believe that the tiny, seemingly insignificant witness we make is precious in His sight.

Many of us read Isaiah's great passage and think we need to be eagles, while most of us are sparrows.

> They who wait for the LORD shall renew their strength, they shall mount up with wings like eagles, they shall run and not be weary, they shall walk and not faint (Is. 40:31).

We see ourselves soaring high in the heady atmosphere with great strong wings, ambassadors to godless people in huge auditoriums or before thousands in some pagan land.

Yes, God needs eagles and they really are spectacular and unusual creatures. But when we realize He didn't make very many eagles, we at least try to be a hawk. After all, they soar high, too.

But most people never learn to fly high, so they frantically try to be something else other than what they are—perhaps songbirds. After all, everyone likes them.

But those who mature along the way often learn to just let the eagles fly and start out to do what sparrows do, for let's face it, most of us are sparrows!

Then, to their joy, they find that sparrows are simply true to the nature God gave them. Besides, He made more of them than any other bird on this continent, when you count the grosbeaks, finches, and buntings.

They are highly migratory and erratic wan-
derers. Nothing comes easy for them; they have to
nest anywhere they can find a place, and they
scrounge for their food like no other bird. And even
though they are not trained to sing, they chirp a lot.
If you listen closely, you'll find it's more beautiful
than all those fancy songs the strutting birds sing.
Come to think about it — I never heard a solo by an
eagle, did you? And besides, who ever saw a sad
sparrow?

God said as nice a thing about them as He did
about Isaiah's eagle: "And not one of them [spar-
rows] is forgotten before God" (Luke 12:6).

I'm saying that in God's eyes it's as grand a thing
to be a sparrow as it is an eagle!

"Being a sparrow" is a good way to describe what
it means to give your witness away by just "doing
your thing." You hold on to your spiritual happiness
by just loving God and scattering your little seeds in
your own little way wherever you go.

If we're eagles we do our "eagle thing," and if
we're sparrows we do our "sparrow thing" — and
God will use it all. He will use anything we'll give
Him. We should know that from the miracle of the
loaves and fishes.

There was a woman whose "thing" was baking
pies. I'm sure that when she baked a fresh lemon pie
and the aroma arose, the angels of heaven looked
over the parapets and licked their heavenly lips
with angelic wistfulness.

If anyone got sick, had a fire, broke a leg, or had a
death in the family she would bake them a lemon
pie. She would knock on their door, and if she didn't

know them she'd say, "I'm Mrs. Ernestine Brown and I'm from the Lord's church. I've brought you a pie." Just another sparrow scattering her seeds, spending her spiritual happiness so she could keep it.

One way you can spend yours is by being a "name-dropper." There is power in the name of the Lord. It is the "name which is above every name" (Phil. 2:9).

A name-dropper, of course, is a person who makes a point of mentioning he knows or has been associated with some nationally known personality, in order to impress others. But Christians can use this technique for God's glory and from completely different motives. It is one of God's most important seeds, so we sparrows ought to scatter plenty of them.

And it is so easy.

The other day I went into a little convenience store. While the man was sacking up my purchase, I casually said, "Well, the Lord did a great job making this day, didn't He?" He never answered, his face didn't change expression, and he never indicated that he heard me, but I know he did.

I drove off with a sparrow song in my heart and committed the man to God. I don't know what happened in that man's mind, but I know what could have happened. The Holy Spirit could have gone right to work on him, and his thoughts could have gone something like this.

The Lord. He mentioned the Lord. My mother loved the Lord and she tried to teach me to love Him. But we certainly have gotten away from Him. Maybe that's why our marriage is so rocky; maybe that's why our teen-agers are giving us so much trouble; maybe that's why I feel so gloomy so much of the time. The Lord. I'm going to talk with my wife about it. Maybe this is the answer. Maybe the church is where we can find what we all need.

I don't know if this happened in his mind, but it's possible. I left a powerful, fertile seed—the Name. It doesn't need much watering to begin to grow.

You can spend beyond your means because God is extravagant with His seeds—He has plenty more where those came from. The River is not going to dry up. He has left us all kinds of obvious signs of His extravagance. Jesus said some seeds will fall on rocky ground; they sprout but the sun wilts them. Some fall on thorny ground and don't grow at all. But a few fall on fertile ground and a bountiful harvest results (see Matt. 13:3-8). He has seeds to spare.

God is extravagant and generous. He has plenty to spend. From Faith House, where we live, down to the main road is about a mile. Between the house and the main road there are at least a hundred thousand black-eyed Susans, maybe more. I expect a few hundred would do, but God is not a seed saver, so He let them fly around and land in droves along our road.

I assume we could have gotten along with just a few dozen species of butterflies, but He made more than seventy-five thousand. Anyone can look up and see that a few thousand stars would have been enough, but there are sixty to seventy million of them in the Milky Way galaxy alone. And we know there are at least a hundred million galaxies!

Twelve years ago our country launched a satellite that flew past Mars and Jupiter and the other planets and sent back marvelous pictures. But it took twelve years at a speed of about thirty thousand miles per hour to fly to the edge of our solar system. Compared to our universe, our little solar system is like a B.B. shot flying around in a space the size of Texas. And we know there are many other universes besides ours. We don't have to worry about God running out of resources!

Accept the fact that some of your seeds may never sprout. That's not your problem. God is a spendthrift; He has plenty more. There is no need for us to go on a seed-conservation kick. I say fling them about with abandon! To do so is to preserve your spiritual happiness. It is the best way I know to assure a lidless well. Besides, it gives the Holy Spirit many wonderful opportunities He otherwise would not have.

"Miss Martha" (that's my pet name for my wife) could never possibly confront a stranger face to face with the claims of Jesus Christ, but she does "her thing." She is a seed-scatterer who has few equals, in my opinion. What a sparrow she is!

If there is a death in a friend's family, she bakes something and takes it over. On one occasion a woman moved to our town who was very ill with cancer, although she was still able to be about.

She joined Martha's prayer group, but was only able to attend twice. Weeks passed, and finally the news came that she had died. Martha baked a cake and I drove her across town to the home of this woman whom she had only met twice.

The door was answered by a heartbroken husband she had never met, and she went inside with her cake to comfort him and two grieving teenagers. When she left that night, that family knew something of the love and compassion of her Lord, transmitted through a caring person and a chocolate cake.

She dropped a fertile seed there, for today that husband is a "turned-on" follower of the Lord Jesus Christ, whereas previously his commitment had been nominal at best. I know in my heart that God grew the seed Miss Martha left that dark night several years ago.

God didn't populate the earth with many eagles, but He certainly filled it with sparrows. If only His sparrows are the faithful seed-scatterers He ordained them to be, the harvest will be greater than we shall ever know this side of eternity.

To keep that happiness, that serenity, that deep blessing of the Presence, we must give it away. Don't worry about stretching God's supply, for He is extravagant. He is so extravagant that He spent *Himself* completely. Then He said to an unhappy world, "Because I live, you will live also" (John 14:19).

Thus the spending of the self for the sake of the beloved is the secret of spiritual happiness, the by-product of the River within. The way to keep the well lidless and the River flowing lies in the spending of this happiness, in the sharing.

So what is your ministry for Him? What witness are you making? If you don't have a ministry for Him, it is probably because you have not asked Him to give you one. It may be He wants you to be a cake-baker, or a phone-caller, or a postcard-writer to shut-ins. It may be He wants you to be a constant name-dropper or an inviter, or just to become a son or daughter to that lonely old person who lives down the block from you. I don't know what He has in mind for you; I only know what He wants from me.

But whether He has eagle work or sparrow tasks, it will be blessed unto you and Him. I know that.

Of course, you are blessed and it is super if you are one of those who can witness in the "conventional" way, if you are the kind who is always ready to present the claims of Christ to perfect strangers.

My friend John Riley is like that. To John, witnessing is like eating. Just as some folks need three meals a day and a few snacks in between, John's day isn't complete unless he has presented the claims of Christ to a half-dozen people or so.

Once we went into an ice-cream parlor for a cone. "You sit at a table and I'll get the cones," he said. So I sat down at a table and got out some notes to scan. After a while I began to wonder why it was taking him so long to get two ice-cream cones. When I looked up, John was in earnest conversation with the young man who had dipped the cones (which were now melting).

He came over and sat down, saying, "I found out that young man is a Christian, so I figured he'd like to talk about Jesus for a while — that's what took me so long."

I say it again: not everybody can be that bold to strangers, but *everyone can be a witness.* And right here I hear the cry again, "I know you said we sparrows were to begin by doing 'our thing,' but I'm too much of an introvert. My faith is such a personal thing. I just can't do it!"

In the first place, don't ever say "I can't" about *anything!* When you say that, your free choice just blocked the Holy Spirit. That phrase never came from the lips of your Savior because it never lodged in His heart.

Besides, you can!

The principal of a junior-high school shared this story with me. There was a student named Henry Boehmer (not his real name). Henry was a very simple young man, an extremely slow learner who possibly had a learning disability that had never been tested and recognized.

Every morning at the opening of the day, a selected student gave a "thought for the day" over the school's public-address system. One day Henry approached the principal and asked if he could give the thought the following morning. The principal was surprised, for Henry was very shy and seldom spoke to anyone.

He said, "To tell the truth, I was a bit surprised that I said yes, but Henry was a Christian and a good boy, so I told him he could do it."

The next morning Henry stepped up to the microphone and, without any book or notes in his hand, said:

Isn't it strange that princes and kings,
And clowns that caper in sawdust rings,
And common folks like you and me are builders for
    eternity?

107

To each is given a bag of tools, a shapeless mass and
   a book of rules,
And each must build 'ere life has flown,
A stumbling block — or a stepping stone.
(Author unknown)

The principal said, "Henry turned and took hold of my arm. I could feel his body trembling. Then he asked, 'Did I do good, Mr. Miller? Did I do good?' "

Mr. Miller put his arm about him and said, "Yes, Henry, you did good — real good!"

When I heard that, I thought about some future day when we will stand before the King — all of us little sparrows and a few songbirds. Then, oh then, I want to hear the King say, "Well done, good and faithful servant. You did good!"

Never again say "I can't." The improbable and the impossible look exactly alike to God.

Somewhere in the vicinity of Colorado Springs there runs up the mountain a tortuously winding road. Along the way you come to a spot so narrow that it appears impossible that a car can make it through.

When you approach that spot a big sign proclaims, "YES, YOU CAN! A MILLION OTHERS HAVE!"

Yes, indeed we can, and we *must* find a way to witness, minister, and give of ourselves if the water within us that springs up into everlasting life is to remain fresh and pure. So give it away!

Lane Adams tells how he once was flying across the South Pacific at about thirty-eight thousand feet. It was a beautiful day with a few wispy clouds floating about far below.

"As we flew along I was watching the vast panorama—you could probably see for a hundred miles. Then, far off to my right, I could see a tiny little dark cloud. It didn't look much larger than my hand, but you could see the water just pouring from it.

"So I said to it, 'Little cloud, why are you doing that? You are so small and this ocean is so big, and there is no land there to receive your rain. You are wasting yourself and your time. That little thing you are doing will do no good whatsoever.' "

Then he said, "I fancied I heard the little cloud's answer drifting back up to me. It said, 'You're wrong; this is not waste—for when I am finished, the ocean will be a little fuller than it was!' "

That's the best reason I ever heard for being extravagant with our witness, no matter how small it may seem to be. Your witness will be an encouragement, and this unhappy world never needed encouraging more than it does today. One of Paul's preachers was named Barnabas. I was thrilled when I discovered that "Barnabas" means, "son of encouragement." Sometimes I wish I were named Barnabas, don't you? Oh, how I want to be an encourager!

I have been saying for a long time that there are some things God, by His own self-limitation, cannot do until He finds people who will pray and release His power. That is because He respects our free choice. Now I want to say that there are also some things that God, by His own self-limitation, cannot do until He finds eagles and sparrows who will be His instruments and witness for Him.

Sometimes the consequences of failing to pray can be tragic, and the same is true of witnessing. If we don't give our spiritual happiness away in some form or another, there are indeed sad and many times calamitous consequences. It is a tragedy indeed when the Holy Spirit is blocked by our failure to do what He has asked.

You and I simply must abandon our "eagle complexes," which tell us that the only witnessing that counts is the grand and the spectacular.

I believe the Lord Jesus tried to teach us that in His resurrection. He lay in the tomb for three days. Then life energy of Almighty God was infused into His still form. Life has stirred through His body. He sat up, then He stood, and what was the first thing He did?

If *I* had just been crucified for the sins of the whole world, and if God had just poured life back into *my* body, I probably would have burst from the tomb in search of a podium from which to make the grand announcement.

But not Jesus. The first thing He did was to take the time to fold very carefully and neatly the napkin that had been bound about His head!

John's account says, "And the napkin, that was about his head, not lying with the linen clothes, but wrapped together in a place by itself" (John 20:7, KJV).

The New King James Bible says the cloth was "folded." Think of it! The Son of God had just blasted death and blown the roof off of human despair, and the very first thing He does is to take the time to fold a napkin neatly! I probably would have thrown it in a crumpled heap in the corner in my haste to get out of that tomb!

That says to me that equally important with the big spectacular things that are done in His name are the number of napkins we have folded along the way—the little, ordinary, commonplace acts of witness that we have done in His name and for His sake.

"Whoever gives to one of these little ones a cup of cold water because he is a disciple, truly, I say to you, he shall not lose his reward" (Matt. 10:42).

folding the napkin

The key phrase here is *because he is a disciple.* The person gives the cup of cold water—or performs some other loving act—because he is a follower of the Lord Jesus Christ.

A friend took the trouble to mail me a book he thought I would enjoy. A neighbor volunteered to pick up the newspapers in our driveway while we were gone. A former student wrote to tell me that she was greatly indebted because of a kindness I happened to show her once, a tiny little act that I had completely forgotten. These people folded those napkins "because they were disciples."

The Lord Jesus Christ came crashing into the life of Mary Snyder, a dear sister in Christ, and changed her into one of the greatest napkin-folders I have ever known.

Our church adopted a Vietnamese family after the Vietnam War. Actually, it would be more accurate to say that Jack and Mary Snyder adopted them. They loved that poor frightened family into strong, productive citizens of this country. She also does regular volunteer work at the hospital. At almost every social function of our church you can find Mary in the kitchen. She and her husband regularly go to a local nursing home to take a handicapped elderly person out to a restaurant to eat. She also does a huge amount of volunteer secretarial work for our particular ministry. There's much more, but that will suffice.

Why does Mary Snyder do these things? "Because she is a disciple," and disciples take the time and trouble to stop amidst all the big things of life to fold napkins for His sake along the way.

All you fellow sparrows, take heart! In the sight of God your witness stands tall alongside the witness of the great saints of the ages. And when our works are reviewed in heaven, I cannot imagine that the King of Glory will ever ask, "What mountains did you climb for Me? What vast kingdoms of Satan did you overthrow? How many great cities did you take for Christ?" But rather, I am certain He will want to know, "How many napkins did you fold along the way, simply because you love Me?"

Never a day will pass when we will not have opportunity to spend our precious spiritual happiness for the sake of someone else.

The world is simply full of rumpled napkins that need folding!

8

Have You Risked Reacting to Reality?

If there ever is a time when you will need to take a "deep-well look" at the River of water within you that "springs up into everlasting life," it is when you decide that once and for all you are going to turn your Christian faith loose to operate in every hard situation you are called upon to face.

That is what I call "risking reality."

It is easy to let love work in the small situations. Your child comes in with a bee sting while you are stirring seven-minute icing. Your phone keeps ringing when you are trying to concentrate on something else. You are in a hurry but someone stops you on the street and wants to talk.

When I say it is "easy," I mean that after the first wave of perfectly natural human annoyance sweeps over us, the mature disciple should be able to step back and quickly get things into focus again, and deal with the situation in a loving, Christlike way.

But what about the big, threatening, seemingly impossible situations? You are accused unjustly; you lose your job; someone else gets the big promotion you deserved; you realize there is malicious gossip about you floating around and it is all blatantly false. What then? Do you "risk reality" here? I mean, do you take the deep-well look, find the inner strength and faith you need, and then proceed to turn the Holy Spirit loose in the midst of the situation?

Or do you retreat into the illusion that if you don't look after number one, no one else is going to? Do you give in to the lie the enemy feeds you that you need to strike back, defend yourself, reply in kind, and give a dose of the same medicine someone gave you?

Spiritual happiness is produced and proven when a person has decided to go Christ's way all the way. After all, He lived in the midst of the same kind of world we live in—it was only culturally different. It, too, was an unhappy world. The world has always been basically unhappy ever since Adam and Eve disobeyed and sin entered the world. Human nature and human emotions have always been the same, which is to say that basic human problems have always been the same.

They lied about Him and twisted His words. They sneered at Him because He ran with the "wrong crowd"; they called Him a troublemaker. They said He was mentally sick (had demons), that He was a nobody because of where He came from, and they turned on Him because He had the courage to be honest. And in the wilderness, the enemy tried to get Him to live His life in fantasy and unreality by giving in to greed for material things and by sacrificing His convictions for the reward of personal popularity.

But Jesus preferred to risk living in reality — the ultimate reality — by thrusting the love of the Father into *every* situation.

What did it get Him? Well, it got Him crucified, but more than that, it got Him spiritual happiness! How do I know? Because just a few hours before He would hang bleeding and dying in the scorching Palestinian sunlight, He told His disciples:

Peace I leave with you; my peace I give to you; not as the world gives do I give to you. Let not your hearts be troubled, neither let them be afraid (John 14:27).

How could He say that? Well, if we can see clearly what Paul saw, we will know the answer to that, for he said, "He is our peace" (Eph. 2:14).

When we boil all that down to everyday terms, it just about wraps up everything we have learned so far on the journey. It simply means that Jesus Himself, through the Holy Spirit, is the River of water that runs beneath the deep well of our circumstances. Affirmation of this can be found in Colossians 1:27 where we find the phrase, "Christ in you, the hope of glory."

It is *that* reality that we must risk applying to our circumstances in this unhappy world. That is what is truly risky — so risky it can even get us crucified!

The enemy is still with us here in the wilderness of this world, trying to get us to avoid spiritual reality and its risk, and to compromise by living in fantasy.

What are the realities we must be prepared to accept?

Reality #1: We have to live in an unhappy world.

We have mentioned this several times, but it is so very vital that we must zero in on it once more. The unhappy world goes all out to tempt us to live in fantasy. All about us the trumpets are sounding announcements that promise blissful living and prosperity for all. They herald that a certain political party, deodorant, house, home computer, video player, or hairdo will bring us Cloud-Nine living and solve most of our problems, and that there will be no spiritual decisions to make. We can just live happily ever afterward.

That is a fantasy world where guns turn into magic wands, credit card bills never come due, malignant bacteria roll over and play dead, and the tooth fairy brings you everything you want without having to work for it! Just pay for it all with a small down payment and easy monthly terms.

Jesus Christ lived in that kind of a world, but it never managed to pour Him into its mold. He was not crucified because He said, "Consider the lilies of the field, how they grow," but because He said, "Consider the thieves of the temple, how they steal." Jesus operated in the real world and spread love through it. He took that risk.

That is where we must live, too—in a world where millions of people are defeated by life. My soul was pierced one day when a lady said, "Well, I suppose I'll just kill another day." She had given up on it all.

It is not an easy thing for a Christian to live in an unhappy world on Monday morning when the church doors are closed and the organ is locked, but we must. It is not an easy thing to turn the Holy Spirit loose to live out the Christlike life in us in each situation that comes along. It is risky business, and there are certain to be times when everyone else thinks you are a fool.

Mother Teresa went down into the slums of India to give her life to the wretched. It is told that some of her friends advised her, "Don't do this. There are missionaries to go and do these things. Just stay here in the convent and you can have a rich, quiet life with us and the Lord."

And when she answered, "But I must go," they asked, "But why?" Well, she didn't answer, "Because if I go, I just might possibly win a Nobel Peace Prize someday."

Instead she answered, "Why must I go? Because the love of Christ constrains me!" I say that was risky business!

And you and I have to come to terms with the reality that while we may not go to some far-off land to serve the Lord, we must risk involvement in the real world here where we live, where sin and lostness abound, where alienation and vulgarities run raw in the streets like broken sewers, where power structures bleed people from their political temples.

We also have to risk letting the Holy Spirit live

117

out a Christlike life in us when there are neighbors who are fussy, husbands who are tired and cross, bosses who are crabby, children who stay in the bathroom eternally, dogs that bark at night and ruin our shrubbery by day, and cars that squeal their tires at 2:00 A.M. in front of the house. It is in these situations that our inner spiritual happiness empowers us to live in victory.

We cannot separate the sacred from the secular, for we have to live *in* the world. And if we think we can permanently withdraw into isolated clusters with a few of our friends and just "have experiences in the Lord" most of the time, we have just parachuted out of the world into Fantasyland.

A man stood up in a meeting and said, "I don't have any problem trusting God and believing He is with me when I'm with friends like you. When someone stands and sings, 'Because He lives, I can face tomorrow,' I'm not afraid of anything. But when I get home and get to thinking about all that I have to do next week, it scares me silly!"

All of us knew what he was talking about. It's asking a lot to be called on to risk everything on the unseen Presence in me and ask Him to live His life through me in *all* my situations.

After all, how can the Holy Spirit spend His time helping me find an apartment or try a new recipe when it is already 4:00 P.M.? Isn't He too busy healing people and wrestling with sin in the cities to bother with questions like, "Should I go swimming with the kids or wax the kitchen floor?" Would He really care about bee-stung fingers?

Can I really believe He would have time for decisions like "Which investments should I make?" or "Should I go into debt for that new car?" or "Do I *actually* need to go back and apologize to that waitress?" How about, "Which one of my children needs my attention most just now?" or "Should I pry a bit and find out what is bugging the fellow who works next to me?" Yes, I know these are important things but they are so *everyday*!

We should not need to be reminded that Jesus didn't spend much time speaking about the "big" things. He mostly talked about life itself—and almost always in *everyday* terms, in terms of folded napkins.

There are no "big" things as such to our heavenly Father, and there are no "small things." There are only valuable things that He has made. Jesus used terms like tables, towels, salt, light, fields, crops, garments, bread, work, lilies, boats, mountains, coins, and dirty feet. How much more *everyday* can you get?

Our place of habitat is not in a grand, insulated carriage with drawn curtains that rolls through the streets of life toward some pointless destination. Our place is right in the midst of this miserable, unhappy world, walking through situation after situation under the lordship and power of the River within us.

Reality #2: The River gives us problems.
Another reality that we must accept and risk is that if we have the River within us, it is going to give us problems. A river is not a docile thing. It has a mind of its own; it cuts its own course, and contains

whirlpools and eddies. Sometimes it floods and overwhelms its environment. If you have the River, you have some problems. But most people begin the Christian journey by thinking otherwise.

Recently a radio evangelist read a letter from a young man:

> I became a Christian a few months ago and for a while it was all so great. The glow was terrific and my friends all knew something super had happened to me. Then it all began to fade away. My friends were all so wrapped up in trying to win others they forgot about me, so I drifted back into my old ways. I have given my life back to Jesus Christ many times, but it seems it is of no use. *I have just as many problems as I ever had!*

That last sentence jarred me. We need to make clear that the kind of peace Jesus gives His followers is the kind He had—peace *amidst the problems*. If the Holy Spirit is going to live out the life of Christ in us, we are not only going to have spiritual happiness, but *we are going to have problems*. We are going to have problems we *never* had when we were spiritually dead!

We are going to have problems with our enemies. If we turn the Holy Spirit loose, He is going to start loving them. We will have problems with those who persecute us, revile us, and despitefully use us; turn Christ loose to live out His life through us and He will start blessing them and praying for them.

Wow! You had problems before? Well, you're going to have a fresh batch! When someone slaps your cheek, you know what the Christ within is going to do, don't you? And what about the kids down the street who constantly cut across your nice lawn? You finally told their father off about it and came home and bragged to your wife about it because it made you feel tall. Turn the River loose in that situation and you will have a *big* problem.

She lied about you. It would be nicer to call it something else, but actually it was a barefaced lie. How did you react? Did you risk reality, or did you handle that one yourself?

When you become a Christian you not only still have many of your old problems, but on top of that you now have problems you never had before!

But you have something else you never had before—you have *Him* and He is the Lord of all things. You have the River within! Deep down, you know He is more than enough.

The struggle exists because our senses tell us that in our humdrum, everyday lives we don't need the River most of the time. Of course, when Junior wakes up in the night with appendicitis, or the Dow-Jones average slips, or Susie starts smoking pot, we need Him in a hurry! But that's different. Otherwise, common sense can handle most of our situations. That is what fantasy will tell us.

But there's not much immediate risk to that. What is risky is that even though the Lord does not work for the IRS, would it cause any problems if He audited every last one of your business deductions? And what about that guy who cut in front of you across five lanes of traffic at seventy-five miles per hour? Did you let the River loose in that situation?

Did you risk reality by praying for him even though your life was spared only by a matter of inches? It is tough to bless those who despitefully use you!

Yes, when you drink of the water Jesus Christ gives you and He becomes a well of water within you springing up into everlasting life, you are going to have problems of loving when everything in you is telling you to do otherwise.

Reality #3: We cannot love only selected people.

What a fantasy it is to think that we can have our own little select group of people and love them to the exclusion of the rest of the world. It is an inviting trap into which God's people all too easily fall.

But John 3:16 ("God so loved the *world*") doesn't refer to a provincial, limited, circle-type of love that has no compassion for the great masses of mankind.

Because that vast army of unknown people seems so far away, so detached from our little sphere, they seem to be only ghostlike non-people parading their misery, hunger, wars, and poverty across a twenty-one-inch TV screen. They actually seem to cease to exist when we turn the news off. But they are real persons who are loved by God, nevertheless.

It is interesting and revealing to me that when Jesus told the parable of the Good Samaritan, he did not slap a label on the victim who lay in the ditch. He simply said, "A *certain man* went down from Jerusalem to Jericho, and fell among thieves" (Luke 10:30, KJV, italics mine).

He did not say if the man was good or bad; if he was Samaritan, Jew, or Gentile; whether he had

122

much wealth or was on government welfare; if he had a Ph.D. or was an eighth-grade graduate; if he was a doctor, lawyer, farmer, blue-collar, or white-collar worker. He did not tell us if he was young or old; married or single; Methodist, Baptist, Presbyterian, or Pentecostal. He did not let us know if he believed in sprinkling or immersion, or if he was a footwasher.

He simply said "a certain man," and the parable makes clear that all of the hurting, unlovely, strange-believing, lost people of this world are to be loved by Jesus Christ through you and me.

If you have never been moved by newscast pictures of starving children in Cambodia or strewn bodies of young men on senseless battlefields, then you may need to ask God for the gift of compassion. He will give it to us if we pray for it until it becomes a real desire in us.

But let's bring it down to the little area where we live. It is fantasy to suppose that we can love only the beautiful people we see. We are so body-oriented here in America; on all sides we are bombarded with propaganda that says "beautiful" means to have a young, movie-star face with the figure of a fashion model or a swimming champion.

But God does not look first at the body. My Bible says, "Man looks on the outward appearance, but the LORD looks on the heart" (1 Sam. 16:7).

One of the most beautiful women I ever knew would rate about a one on a scale of one to ten—if you only looked at her body, that is. She was bedfast, emaciated, thin, with great hollow eyes and sunken cheeks. But what a spirit she had—what a beautiful, gorgeous, deep irresistible charisma of the soul!

If we loved people according to their inner beauty, Miss America might flash her radiant smile from a wheelchair. I'm saying that if we think we can screen out the physically unattractive people (yes, even the ugly), we live in fantasy and the lid will slide across our well-top.

We can even have this attitude and not be aware of it. If all our loved ones must be "like us," then we are in trouble. We certainly would have had trouble loving some of the characters in the Bible.

For instance, Isaiah once went walking down the street naked. If there was ever a bleeding heart, it was Jeremiah. Hosea had bad marital problems. Ezekiel was a strange-eyed mystic who bored through walls and performed sword-dances in public!

Further, the idea is prevalent among many younger people that "senior citizens" also have been transformed somehow into non-persons who no longer enjoy hugs and kisses or the ravishingly beautiful things of the creations, simply because their faces have grown wrinkled and their backs are stooped.

Others have the notion that poverty-stricken people are so concerned with filling their stomachs that they simply do not love as much as the more affluent.

Then there are the robbers, the rapists, the drug addicts, the misfits, and the derelicts and winos who haunt inner-city missions. The idea unconsciously seeps into our minds that these are people we are not required to love. Therefore we can just discard them in some kind of trash bag of unreality, and Monday morning they will be hauled away with the rest of the unwanted refuse of the world.

It seems a bit trite to say, perhaps, but in reality no one ever stops being *human*. Therefore, the need to be loved and wanted never disappears, no matter what kind of conduct masks it.

We simply need to remember that Jesus Christ considers *everybody* worthy of His love. He is never distracted by what we *do* because He always remembers who we *are*. He is always going out on the wild mountainsides after wet, defeated, lost sheep and bringing them home.

So you see, when John the revelator wrote in the Spirit, "Whosoever will, let him take the water of life freely" (Rev. 22:17, KJV), he didn't just mean that nice family in the suburbs with the neat lawn and adorable house; he meant *anyone*! Oh, how I wish all of God's children could really, really believe that!

The point is that externals mean nothing. We are *all* in the same boat, and that is why we cannot select the people we want to love. They all are equal in the sight of God.

To love does not mean "to like, admire, or be attracted to." We are not required to do all those things. With four and a half billion of us moving about on this planet just now, there is no way all personality types are going to become mutual admiration societies.

But if we turn Christ loose in us (through the Holy Spirit) to live out His life, then we are going to see that God "shows no partiality" (Acts 10:34).

Jesus did not love only those whose theology conformed to His. He never loved anyone on the basis of what they believed. When we reach the point where we can reject what a person believes and what he does without rejecting the *person*, then we will have begun to grow some spiritual muscles.

When you get right down to it, it really is some kind of a huge risk to go out on a limb for Him who upholds the universe by His Word of power (see Heb. 1:3)!

But as everybody knows, out on the limb is where the fruit is!

Reality #4: He never leaves us.

This is the most blessed reality about living in this unhappy world. There is a verse of Scripture that I placed on the wall of my study because I constantly need to be reminded of what it tells me:

As I was with Moses, so I will be with you;
I will not fail you or forsake you (Josh. 1:5).

I placed it there because of the struggle I have to keep things in perspective. I need it there because I am still learning not to live by my *feelings* about what is happening but by *what God says* about what is happening.

I suppose the one cry from other Christians I have heard most in my lifetime is, "I feel as if God has left me." But the blessed reality is that He *never* leaves us. Perhaps it will encourage some if I say that I rarely feel that way anymore, for now I know about the deep-well look. And when that feeling begins to creep into my circumstances, I stop for a while and look down deep, through all the darkness of the depths, and I find that the awesome, majestic, yet tender and tremendously personal River is still there!

I just have to say "Glory!"

Most people begin to feel as if they have been forsaken by Him when they don't get quick answers to their prayers or right-now solutions to their problems.

It has been my experience—and that of many, many of the personalities who march through the pages of the Bible—that God seldom grants quick solutions.

God let Noah drift around out there on that vast sea of water for almost a *year*! And after the dove came back with that little green symbol of life in her beak, it was eighty-seven more days before they spotted land!

Did you say you wanted God to give you the solution to your problem by 3:00 P.M. this afternoon?

God let Moses mellow for forty years in the Midianite desert before he finally was ripe enough to come out from the sheep flock and be who God meant him to be.

After Paul was blinded on the Damascus road, when he met the Lord Jesus Christ face to face, it was several years before he was given a green light for his missionary journeys.

Jesus rebuked the disciples when they wanted to call down immediate fire on a city that had rejected the gospel.

So the Bible makes it abundantly clear that God

takes His own sweet time before He gives answers and solutions, if indeed He gives them at all.

The creation amply illustrates that God doesn't specialize in quick answers or right-now solutions. A mushroom in the forest can grow to the size of a softball overnight. A horseweed can grow to six feet in height in a few days. Hundreds of thousands of acres of clouds can form in a few hours, and disappear overnight. None of these things last.

It seems as if we ought to get the message that when God wants to grow something and preserve it amidst and against difficulties, He takes His time! If you are not convinced, take a look at the great forests of giant redwood and sequoia trees.

Sometimes He does give quick answers and solutions, but generally speaking we have to wait Him out. He knows that waiting builds and strengthens faith when we finally see what He was waiting to bring about.

Whatever it is in your heart that is begging for a quick answer, whatever it is that is eating away your happiness, look down in your well and find rest, for the River is faithful and still flowing. God may not meet our schedule, but He is always on time!

He never leaves us. That is not some kind of escapist self-delusion, but blessed reality—inescapable truth.

There came a time in my life when I entered into what many Christians call a "dry spell." It seemed as if the pressure and burdens of my job were so demanding that the harder I tried the further behind I got.

There were a hundred little tasks I knew I'd

never get done. There were a hundred visits to people in need that I knew would never get made. There were a hundred books I knew would never get read.

Gradually and stealthily, the enemy pulled the plug on my spiritual serenity, and for several days I went about listlessly, without enthusiasm and in a state of mild depression and anxiety.

One summer afternoon after lunch I started out to begin my afternoon tasks, not because I was motivated but simply out of a feeling of duty. I stepped out on the front porch and suddenly, unexpectedly, it seemed the Holy Spirit welled up within me and said, "Wait for a moment."

I stopped, and from across town there came a message from a church steeple as its carillon chimes played a hymn. Through the power of the Lord to use whatever medium He chooses, He quickened the words of the old hymn "His Eye Is on the Sparrow" with the blazing fire of certainty that they were spoken out of His great heart to mine. Here is what they said:

Why should I feel discouraged,
    Whenever shadows come?
Why should my heart be lonely
    And long for heaven and home?
When Jesus is my portion,
    My constant friend is He,
His eye is on the sparrow —
    And I know He watches me.

Then it was as if He put his arm around me and

whispered, "My child, for a while you forgot that I said I'd never leave you nor forsake you, didn't you? See—you were wrong!"

And when He said that, there swept over me a mighty tidal wave of glorious affirmation and certainty; and all the listlessness, the depression, and the burdens were just washed away by the mighty onslaught of the River. Spiritual happiness exploded within me, and I went praising and singing out into the afternoon.

Yes, it is risky business to let Jesus Christ live out His life in you in the midst of an unhappy world like this. But here is one no-risk truth, and you can count on it.

He never leaves us!

9

See the River Flow!

We are not meant to live on mountain peaks; the air is too heady up there; and there is little growth above the timberline. We are meant to live down the mountain a bit, but our wells were drilled to enjoy the never-ending luxury of being full. We know this is true because Jesus said of anyone who will let Him drill a well in their lives: "The water that I shall give him will become in him a spring of water welling up to eternal life" (John 4:14).

That does not mean we'll go about shooting spiritual laser beams and gamma rays, but it does mean that the awesome power of the Lord God will be constantly at work. "For God is at work in you, both to will and to work for his good pleasure" (Phil. 2:13).

Most of the time we are not able to see those workings. He wisely planned it this way in order for us to learn what it means to live by faith. But from time to time, because He loves us and because He wants to encourage us, He gives us a look at the work He is doing in us and in others — a look so clear and obvious that there is no way we can miss seeing it.

Did you ever stop to think that when God created the heavens and the earth, the last creature He formed was man? First He filled the creation with His light. Then He made the firmament, the oceans, vegetation, sun, moon, all living creatures, and last of all He made man.

Knowing ourselves, it ought to be obvious why He worked in that order. If He had made Adam first, he would have been at His elbow all week telling Him just how to do it!

The Holy Spirit within us works day and night. "In everything God works for good" (Rom. 8:28). But He is not always unseen and silent. Sometimes we can see Him. Sometimes the River comes boiling up out of the well so near to the surface that through our eyes of faith we can see such brilliant and astounding maneuvering, and such breathtaking wisdom with such fantastic results, that it simply rips the seams of our glory-valves! Sometimes He just rises out of the well and a flood results. And as Noah could tell us, when God floods it is some kind of flood!

At one time I had the privilege of appearing on a talk show on a Christian TV station in Florida. The person interviewing me was not just a "pro"; he was alive in Christ and we had a great time visiting together.

There were five ladies in the room taking phone calls from viewers, and with about ten minutes to go one of them brought us a stack of prayer requests.

My host read and offered a brief prayer for each one, and then he said, "I have one prayer request left. It's from a viewer who is contemplating suicide! And I just feel led to ask Brother Prater to pray for this person."

So saying, he handed the slip of paper to me.

It was so sudden and unexpected that I didn't have time to block out God with some prepared words that would probably have been inadequate. A great tidal wave of inadequacy swept over me and inwardly I cried out, "O God, O God, help me!"

I wheeled my chair around, looked directly into the eye of the camera, and began to pray for this unknown, desperate, defeated person.

There is no way to describe what happened. Words are completely impotent here. I can only describe how it seemed to me, and trust that every reader will be mature enough to understand.

It was as if there were a large, circular hole in the top of my head and the Holy Spirit was just pouring in His perfect words of comfort, strength, and hope. The words came with power and authority in a calm but deeply communicative manner.

Inwardly I knew that what was being prayed was beautiful and perfect. I was completely detached from the words; I had absolutely nothing to do with the thought origins. It was Christ in me who spoke the words. Therefore, they had to be the exact words this person needed to hear!

And I knew *I had seen the River flow!*

As we drove away from the TV station I was praising and glorifying God, for He had done so much more than I had expected. I had gone down there to promote a book written for His glory, but He had gone with me into the thorns and brambles of the midnight to reach out to that one lost sheep. Spiritual happiness boiled within my heart.

Have you ever seen the River of the Holy Spirit at floodtide, as He rises out of the calm depths of your being where He abides and comes crashing onto the scene of your needs right in the midst of this unhappy world where you live?

Have you seen Him rise up out of other people's wells in times of great need, when they are called upon to do tasks that are too big for them, or when they face brick walls of impossibility and great mountains of stony problems that have no solutions? Then the River comes roaring down the canyons of their lives, and the impossibilities and mountains simply crumble before His onslaught. After the flood there are awesome vistas of needs that have been met and problems that have been worked out.

Have you ever seen the River burst out when tragedy has torn a gaping hole in people's expectations?

I wish you could know Jim Zerkle and his wife, Bev. A former Air Force captain, Jim and Bev are youth sponsors in our church. He also coaches the church softball and basketball teams. The influence and witness they have for our Lord will never be known this side of eternity.

Not long ago, their nineteen-year-old son was driving from a nearby city where he worked when sleep overcame him. His car veered from the road, flipped on its back, and landed in a deep ditch filled with water, where he drowned.

Jim was a veritable pillar of strength. People came to his home to give comfort, and they received it; they came to offer strength, and they left strengthened within themselves. The assurance of the love and presence of God in the lives of Jim and Bev never shone more brightly than it did during those pain-filled hours.

One of his relatives said, "I don't see how he does it. I just don't see how he does it."

But another replied, "Well, Jim opened an account with the Lord a long time ago, and tonight he has been drawing out his interest on it!"

We had all seen the River flowing!

There is no doubt about it. When a person comes to God and offers up to Him his all and asks Jesus Christ to come into his life and take over, *He comes!* That's spiritual happiness!

Now let's just stop a moment to try and take that into our consciousness. Would to God heaven would drop a searing hot bomb of dazzling light into the comprehension centers of our brains and we could be *completely* aware of what that means. Think of it! The life of Jesus Christ *in you*—not just theologically, but *really!*

When I caught a glimpse of the reality of that for the first time, the floodgates of my soul opened wide and I was swept away by billows of rolling, cascading joy mixed with unspeakable awe and delight! I suppose one might say, I *really knew* then what spiritual happiness is.

Sometimes the River reaches flood stage slowly

and gradually, but when you watch Him rolling along in His unchangeable, redemptive purposefulness it is equally awesome.

Let me bring you up to date in the adventure that began that terrifying night when two masked men robbed our home. Remember that since that time one of them has been killed and the other is back in prison.

I ask you to be grown up enough in Christ not to admire us for what I am about to share, but to glorify Him — for what we did is what any committed follower of His would do.

We obtained the name and address of the surviving robber from our local sheriff, and we wrote him where he was being held in Lakewood, Colorado. We sent him some literature and told him that we forgave him because Jesus Christ had forgiven us. We reminded him that for thirty years he had made a mess of his life by trying to run it himself, and we suggested that he receive Christ by faith and turn the rest of his life over to the Lord.

Finally, we told him that we cared about him and loved him with the love of Christ.

He answered immediately, and was genuinely and deeply touched by our witness. Since then we have established a regular every-other-week exchange of letters and have grown to be dear friends together in the Lord, for he has received our Christ and has found a new and exciting life, even behind prison walls.

Let me quote just two or three lines from some of his letters:

See the River Flow!

Since I've accepted Jesus Christ as my Lord and Savior he's done a lot for me. I don't think about my freedom quite as much . . . now whatever happens is all up to him!

This is the man who was party to the beating of a seventy-year-old man! Can you see the River? Here are some more.

When I think of you, I think of myself and you. After all, "We are laborers together with God" (1 Cor. 3:9).

You've helped me so much and I love the both of you through Christ and my mind.

Remember, this is the man who pointed his gun at me for an hour and sneered when I told him I was praying. See the River flow!
He has begun to write poetry.

How precious was the time of my seeking,
    Each moment, each hour of each day.
Oh, I'm so glad that I sought him,
    The Life, the Truth and The Way.

His look was one of compassion,
    His gaze was one of release.
But his touch was one of great mercy,
    For when he touched me, he gave me peace.

Whoever cannot see the River flowing in all of this had better scramble for higher ground, for they are surely in danger of being drowned and swept away!

How sweet and wonderful it is when spiritual happiness is combined with circumstantial happiness, and we ride the flooding River in serenity and joy! Like Paul, our friend is held in man's prisons, but he has never been more free now that he has become a "prisoner of the Lord" (Eph. 4:1).

Have you seen the River flow recently?

Perhaps not. Perhaps in your life there are wounds of sorrow that somehow seem never to heal over. Perhaps there is something you have prayed long about and no answer has come. Perhaps there is some beloved person for whose salvation you have been storming heaven's gates for years. Maybe there is some problem facing you that looms like a great impassable mountain range; there is absolutely no way around that you can see.

Well, I have a word for you: *the River still flows!* In depths of your life that your feelings and senses can never reach, the Lord Jesus Christ is there, working in this unhappy world in the very midst of your doubts and apprehensions. And He is working not just for good answers and solutions, but for the *best* ones for you and your loved ones.

Believe that today! Resolve inwardly that until someone can show you a better way you are going to "cast all your anxieties on him, for he cares about you" (1 Pet. 5:7). Renew your commitment to the God whose last name is not "defeat" but "Omega," and that means that He who began this strange adventure we call life is in complete and absolute charge, and that He will control the end!

Take that lid from the well He dug within you when you were born into the kingdom, and peer long and deep down through the darkness of your circumstances. In due time you will see the River—Jesus Christ through the Holy Spirit—abiding there as He promised.

Then one day the River will rise up, and you will watch Him as He floods through your impenetrable darkness and carries you out into the light again.

What a glorious blessing it is when out of our need He gives us a clear look at His workings.

A few years ago I was one of the participants at a Christian retreat in the Mid-South. One night there kept pressing on me a message I had not planned to deliver. I wrestled with it, argued, and reasoned, but all to no avail—the Lord prevailed. It was a message on forgiveness.

Three years later I was invited back to the same retreat. During that time a woman came to me, took me aside, and said, "I'm sure you don't remember me, but I was here three years ago and I just wanted to thank you for that message on forgiveness. It was for me."

She went on, "I did not like my daughter-in-law. I didn't think she was good enough for my son. I criticized everything she did or tried to do.

"But after the retreat I went home and sought her out. I told her how I had disliked her, how I had wronged her, and I asked for her forgiveness. She forgave me, and we were gloriously reconciled and fell into one another's arms with gladness and love.

"That was in the spring, and in July my son and his wife went down to the lake. She was learning to skin dive, and she waded out into the water and went down. Something happened, and she never came up. She was drowned."

Then her voice broke and tears cascaded down her cheeks, and she said, "Oh, what if you had not brought that message? What if she had died and I had been left with all that poison in my heart? But oh, you did bring that message, and I just want to thank you and tell you that today there is peace in my soul because of it!"

When she said that, the entire fireworks factory of joy within me caught fire and started such a conflagration that the mercury in my hallelujah thermometer went right through the top! Roman candles of Christian happiness tore through my soul. Blockbusters and strings of ladyfingers cracked and popped in the praise section of my brain. Star shells and cherry bombs of thanksgiving raced through my entire being as I celebrated the compassionate goodness of God!

I had seen the River flowing!

Yes, I know it is a sin-cursed, unhappy, wretched world that writhes and groans in its lostness and its feverish, mad rush for self-gratification.

But I know something else. Even though we must live in its midst, there is happiness untold within its boundaries. For Jesus Christ is the complete and absolute Lord of it. He is the River that flows in ultimate and final power through it. There is no defeat in Him, and since He has taken up His dwelling place in us there can be no defeat in us, either. None whatsoever!

That is why we are happy as we press on toward the homeland!

- Michele] breast cancer
- Glenda's sister] — (Chemo
- Cecl's sister ↙

- daughter (Stephanie))
  ido.
- Charlie
- Tim's uncle (leukemia)
- Debbie
- LaDow: Erin